Legacy

Mysteries - Memories - Musings

Wanda Strange

To Carolyn,
Thank you for your
support and love. I have
your own stories,
love,
Wanda Strange
December 2016

Published by

Radical Women (DBA)
PO Box 782
Granbury, TX 76048
www.bylisabell.com

ISBN-13: 978-0998330815
ISBN-10: 0998330817

Dedication
I lovingly dedicate Legacy to
Amy, Ginger, Jenni, Chris, Amber, Diane,
Scott, Kristen, Elizabeth, Mark, Angela.
I love each of you with your unique personalities.
I love that family means so much to you.
Love,
Aunt Wanda

Acknowledgements

I gratefully acknowledge my siblings and cousins who shared stories and sparked additional memories of our family.

Thank you Homer, Brenda, Betty and Jo Ann for the memories of your parents and our grandparents.

Thank you Mike, Patty, and Lisa for your support . You always encourage and support me. This is our collective story.

Thank you Kerry, Ginger, and Beverly for being my sounding board, first line editors, and encouragers.

Special thanks to my sisters: Lisa for hours of tutoring and sharing your expertise and Patty for technical advice and expertise

Legacy

"If you would not be forgotten as soon as you are dead, either write something worth reading or do something worth writing."
Benjamin Franklin

Legacy

"Your story is the greatest legacy that you will leave to your friends. It's the longest-lasting legacy you will leave to your heirs."
Steve Saint
Ecuadorian-born pilot, founder of I-Tec,
and son of martyred missionary, Nate Saint

Heirlooms representing our family history grace many areas of my home. The space above my kitchen cabinets resembles a museum display of practical objects, each evoking special memories of the ancestors who utilized them.

Every morning my Granddaddy poured fresh milk from a bucket into the large Marshall Pottery crock and skimmed cream to fill the matching smaller cream pitcher. A shadow box contains the baby fork and spoon used by my father-in-law, Gerald Ray Strange.

Granny treasured the clown cookie jar, a gift from her oldest grandson, purchased with his first paycheck. Once painted bright green, the buttons and hat barely display their previous color. Granny lovingly repaired the lid after small hands dropped it in a quest for the treats inside. It maintained its prominent place in her kitchen despite missing a chunk of the clown's collar.

I visualize Granmommie Cargile's hands carefully painting in ceramic class at the nursing home as she created the treasured white soup tureen. Two teapots on a shelf in my living room remind me of special summer afternoons with Granny Carr. Just the two of us – I listened as she shared memories – stories she shared with no one else.

A specially designed ladder in the corner of my bedroom displays an assortment of quilts. The collection represents the blending of our families - Granmommie's *Wedding Ring*, Melba's *Sunbonnet Sue,* and Aunt Margaret's *Star Pattern.* In the opposite corner, Momo Dooly's Montgomery Ward sewing machine transports me to childhood days. My little bitty grandmother vigorously peddled the treadle as she stitched the well-used depression era *Patchwork* quilt. The varied patterns demonstrate our grandmothers' individual skills and provide a tangible representation of our merged families.

Many boxes of pictures, letters, and mementos provide clues to the individual owners - all belongings left by the women and men whose DNA flows through my veins. Though no item possesses significant monetary value, the true worth exists in the sentimental value of the memories they evoke.

The concept of inheritance for most people conjures thoughts of money or perhaps property. My ancestors owned little. Conversely, life required backbreaking work, a struggle to survive, and to provide the essentials. Each material possession served a practical purpose. The family rarely purchased luxuries.

Physically, we inherited characteristics from our relatives – the color of our eyes, our body type, genetic predispositions for all kinds of maladies. (Perhaps even the grey streak at our left frontal hairline.)

Beyond an inheritance of material wealth, belongings, or even genetic predispositions, a legacy encompasses everything received from predecessors. Our family left a rich heritage. A history filled with memories and intriguing stories – a legacy based on a strong work ethic, honesty, integrity, commitment to community, devotion to family, and a steadfast faith in God.

Many people measure success by the amount of money, property, or possessions they obtain. An anonymous quote disagrees with this philosophy. "It is not what you gather but what you scatter that tells what kind of life you have lived."

Family shapes us into the people we become. We choose to incorporate the strengths of parents and grandparents. If wise, we learn from the mistakes of the past. The account of my family recalls ordinary people who worked hard to make a good life. No individual achieved fame or fortune. Instead, accounts of difficult circumstances provide examples of facing adversity with strength and grace – or in other cases illustrations of poor choices.

The stories passed down from generation to generation paint a picture of a family history and allow us to understand the character of the men and women whose bloodline we share. My ancestors scattered seeds. Literally, the seeds they sowed resulted in the crops that fed their families. Beyond those literal seeds, they scattered descendants. Though each of us possesses unique personalities, we share similarities and bonds of history and genetics.

As a little girl, I idolized my grandparents, ordinary human beings, far from perfect people, whose stories deserve to be remembered. As I introduce them, I hope the evidence reveals their character. I suspect my family may recognize something of themselves in the idiosyncrasies the stories reveal. I certainly do.

I write to honor my family – to learn more about the lives that shaped their children and grandchildren –to understand their moral fiber and insure their stories and my memories survive beyond our earthly existence.

The Family Tree

George Washington Dooly
1870 – 1955

James Henry Williams
1864 – 1911

William Johnson Carr
1861 – 1912

William S. Tyler
1873 – ?

Sarah Ellen Dupree
1873 -- 1900

Nancy Elizabeth Morgan
1862 -- 1957

Florence Emma Jacobs
1868 – 1955

Jemima Sarah Caldonia Coker
1873 -- 1939

John Bradford Dooly
1892 – 1956

Gladys Virginia Williams
1898 – 1987

John Marion Carr
1892 – 1972

Verna Mary Tyler
1895 – 1984

George Wallace Dooly
1929 – 2007

Wanda Juanita Carr
1933 – 2011

Dooly
Wanda Merle
George Michael
Patricia Inez
Lisa Arlene

Sunday Drive

*"...And at the end of it he knew, and with the knowledge
came the definite sense of new direction toward which he
had long been groping, that the dark ancestral cae, the womb
from which mankind emerged into the light, forever pulls
one back – but that you can't go home again."*
Thomas Wolfe

"Patty, do you have any idea where we're going?"

"I know exactly where it is – sort of?" Patty reassured our spouses as we embarked on a Sunday afternoon adventure.

The farm roads intersected at a familiar site. The abandoned cotton gin assured us we were on the right track. The deteriorating school building, once the center of community activity, served as storage facility for hay. Broken down cars filled the surrounding property giving the appearance of a wrecking yard. The building across the road, previously a general store, no longer provided the gathering place for locals to swap stories. Well past noon, services over and worshippers departed, the little white country church stood as the only well maintained building at the crossroads.

"We're definitely on the right track" my sister and I agreed.

"Turn at the second right" Patty instructed and Mike followed his wife's direction.

"I remember the road curved to the left, past a house on a hill, the farm is on the left. There should be two houses in close proximity." I added.

At the end of the road, it did indeed turn to the left. The road began to curve and wind. Nothing about the area looked familiar.

"Go back and take the first right," I instructed.

Mike retraced our steps as Kerry needled us about knowing "exactly where to find the old home place."

"Be patient! We haven't been here in over 40 years."

As the road curved to the left, the route looked a little more familiar. At the top of the hill, crumbling remains of an old farmhouse stood on the right. "I remember that house. It belonged to the lady who taught piano lessons – I think her name was Mrs. Cross."

Less than a mile down the road, a newer home stood on the site where my Aunt once lived.

"Keep going. I think that's it – those two houses on the left."

My apprehension grew as we approached the area. So many questions – Did I possess the emotional stability to deal with what we found? Would the house still be there at all? Why didn't I pay more attention to my Grandparent's stories? Why didn't I encourage my parents to share their memories?

It appeared so different. A modern RV seemed out of place between the remains of two old farmhouses. We passed the site, turned around, and parked. We positioned the vehicle for a better look to determine if indeed we were in the right place. Stopping on the country road, we attracted the attention of a local couple.

"We think this was our Grandparents' farm," we explained.

"My parents lived here for nine years." The young woman told us.

"I remember the Griffin family bought my grandfather's farm. Their daughter, Lettie, and I used to play together whenever I visited."

"Lettie was my aunt. The family still owns the property and an uncle is staying here in his RV," the young lady filled in details.

"Would it be okay if we looked around?"

"Sure. Watch for snakes." She warned.

No problem. I may be a city girl, but my fear of rattlesnakes borders on phobia, I thought as we said our goodbyes and they drove away.

The remains barely resembled the place of my childhood memories. Gone – the white picket fence surrounding the house. Gone – the beautiful roses and flower gardens. Gone – the fruit orchard and vegetable garden. Gone – a huge Mulberry tree, the source of the most severe discipline of my youth.

What remained? The front room stood precariously, holding memories of my grandparents watching television and entertaining friends and family. A concrete step and slab signaled the location of the back door and patio, and a square area lined with bricks indicated the site of the old well house. We assumed the large piece of metal on the ground covered the cellar. The voice of reason prevented further exploration.

Patty and I walked the property and remembered. Our collective memories reconstructed each building. It seemed so much bigger in my memory.

Standing on the land, a flood of emotions washed over me – sadness for the loss of vitality – nostalgia for things of the past – but strongest of all, joyful thanksgiving for the legacy represented by this land and the family who settled it.

Our family's inheritance cannot be measured in currency, a house, or even land. We inherited a legacy of shared memories, love for each other, a strong work ethic, and an assurance of God's faithfulness.

The remaining structure stood as a testament to my daddy and granddaddy's carpentry skills. They spent many weekends in the late 1950s enclosing the screened-in porch to create a family room. The front door opened into a rectangular room with large windows at each end. When opened, the windows utilized the West Texas wind to create a breeze. At one end of the room, a large "swamp cooler" served as the only air-conditioning for the entire house. The large open-faced box fan with large blades moved air into the room. Straw surrounded the outside of the box creating a barrier from the outdoors. To add moisture to the air, Granddaddy attached a hose to the top of the box. This served to wet the straw. The wind blew over the straw and threw a mist into the room supplying a cool breeze.

In the corner next to the fan, a black and white console television stood. On the opposite wall, a long sofa provided Granddaddy a place to stretch out, watch television, and take his daily nap. Matching rocking recliners, strategically positioned at the opposite end of the room, optimized television viewing.

Parallel to the front door, another opening led to the remainder of the home. The original farmhouse consisted of four rooms. The large square living room housed chairs, an upright piano and allowed space for folding tables. Floral paper decorated the walls, and patterned linoleum covered the floors. The family often gathered in this room to sing, play games, or visit.

Adjacent to the family room, a bedroom offered a double bed for overnight guests. Quilts supplied warmth in the winter, and box fans circulated air in the hot summer. A cedar chest at the end of the bed contained extra quilts and linens. Floral patterned wallpaper covered the bedroom walls. I loved this retreat. At home, I shared a bed with my younger sister and a room with my three siblings. I considered it a treat to sleep in a bed by myself and loved being the center of my grandparent's attention. The room represented a place of solitude and freedom from the responsibilities of being the oldest daughter.

The large kitchen provided the hub of family activities, especially for the women. Granny prepared three substantial meals every day. A hearty breakfast fueled the family for the day's labor. After breakfast, the day's chores began. The males headed to the field, and the women started preparations for lunch. Supporting activities like gathering eggs, picking fruits and vegetables, washing, peeling, and putting away produce consumed a large portion of the day. Granny and Granddaddy grew or produced most of what they ate.

A large table occupied the center of the room and allowed seating for the extended family. On one wall, a long wooden buffet held table linens and provided a surface to serve large family meals. A large pantry held canned goods, as well as the items they purchased at the grocery store in nearby Merkel.

The clock on the wall above the pantry fascinated me. Small, ornately carved figures of a Dutch boy and girl emerged alternately to announce hour. Animated sounds demanded attention and kept the kitchen workers on schedule.

Near the back door, a well supplied water for the kitchen. Initially, the well house pumped water through a hose to the kitchen sink. Daddy used his plumbing skills to modernize Granny's kitchen with running water. As a part of the modernization project, Daddy, Granddaddy, and Uncle Buddy built an indoor bathroom, laundry, and storage room. Granny felt like a lady of leisure when she got an electric washing machine and trips to the outdoor toilet became a memory.

Granny and Granddaddy's bedroom completed the square house. A table separated the two beds in the room. Granddaddy slept in the double bed, and Granny slept in the smaller twin bed. To get to the back door you had to go through their bedroom. Privacy obviously was not a priority.

Verna and John Carr raised seven children in this small farmhouse. Though they enjoyed few luxuries, crops and livestock provided enough to feed and provide for their family.

The farm of my memories included much more than the house and consisted of multiple out buildings. A left turn from the gravel county road revealed an open area for family and guests to park their vehicles. A large garage/workshop housed the family car and Granddaddy's tools. Unless employed in the field, the John Deere tractor occupied a prominent spot under a spreading shade tree.

A white picket fence lined with flowerbeds surrounded the house. Brightly colored metal chairs adorned the lawn. The intense Texas summer heated the chairs to hazard level. Quite often, my bare legs suffered burns from the hot metal seats. After sunset, the chairs cooled quickly and provided a pleasant place for the adults to pass the evenings.

A rotating blade push mower kept the grass neatly cut, and Granny's green thumb assured a variety of flowers. Rose bushes added a pop of color to the flat, desolate West Texas landscape. Just outside the fenced yard an orchard of peach and plum trees shaded the vegetable garden, which provided much of the family's food supply.

Every morning Granny swept the backyard. An area of tightly packed red dirt, devoid of vegetation starkly contrasted with the lush front yard's flowers and the garden's produce. Concrete walkways lead to the well, bathhouse, smokehouse, and a building that served as storage and housed a cottonseed bin.

A windmill topped the well and supplied the energy to pump water for the garden and the house. Adjacent to the well, a bathhouse served as a place for bathing before the installation of indoor plumbing. The hose from the well supplied water to the washtub. By the late 50s, Granny turned the unused washhouse into a playhouse complete with dress up clothes and pretend dishes for my cousin, Jo, and I to enjoy our own pretend world.

We rarely left the safety of the yard without adult supervision. Each building served a specific purpose. The chicken house – the hog pen – the cattle feeding lot – an outhouse. The family dog and multiple cats shared the rural space with snakes and a variety of wild animals.

The Sunday drive stirred bittersweet feelings. Fifty years later none of the buildings remains. No one who knew my grandparents still resides in the area. Like their neighbors, they lived simple quiet and sometimes difficult lives. Each story represents a brick in the building of a family heritage. While the physical buildings deteriorate and eventually cease to exist, the ancestors live beyond their natural lives in shared stories and memories.

Ancestors

"The very essence of our nation is founded on the strength, courage, and determination of these immigrants."
Thomas Jefferson

Roots: The Reality of a Melting Pot

"Consider a tree for a moment. As beautiful as trees are to look at, we don't see what goes on underground - as they grow roots. Trees must develop deep roots in order to grow strong and produce their beauty. But we don't see the roots. We just see and enjoy the beauty. In much the same way, what goes on inside of us is like the roots of a tree."
Joyce Meyer

My Texas roots run deep. Every branch of my family tree arrived in Texas more than a century ago. Though each individual took a different route, their lives intersected in the small west Texas community of Noodle, Texas. Perhaps the promise of affordable land drew the settlers to a desolate place named by the Indians. The Native Americans called the place *nothing*, because the dry creek bed failed to meet the expectations and needs of their people. However, German and Irish immigrants grew to love this land and called it home. They accepted the physically demanding farm labor as a way of life, planted crops, and established roots.

Around the turn of the century, my ancestors migrated to west Texas. Some saw unlimited opportunity in affordable (five-dollar an acre) land. They sought the respect, security, and independence land ownership afforded. Others simply needed work and followed family members to the area. Hard-working sharecroppers dreamed of owning their own land. Believing if they worked hard enough and lived frugally, they could achieve their dream.

If my Texas roots run deep, my American roots run even deeper. Ancestors resided in America before the Revolutionary War. Their various routes led them from Germany, Ireland, Scotland, England, Norway, and Switzerland through Pennsylvania, Virginia, North Carolina, Tennessee, and Missouri. Eventually, they settled in Noodle, Texas.

With the family name of Dooly/Dooley, I proudly claimed my Irish heritage. Family stories also pointed to an Irish connection in the Carr line as well. As a little girl, I listened to stories of connections to Germany. Granny shared stories of her father-in-law, Fritz Deutschman's, immigration from Germany at the turn of the century. Unlike my cousins, I didn't share that lineage. Imagine my surprise to discover an actual ancestral link to Germany in more than one branch of my family tree.

Why immigrants chose to risk everything to make a new life in America requires imagination and speculation. However, history provides clues to explain their willingness to leave the familiar homeland for the challenges of an unknown frontier.

Rampant war, poverty, and religious persecution in the fifteenth and sixteenth centuries caused Western Europeans to seek refuge in America. For more than one-hundred-fifty years, Protestants suffered cruel persecution and death. The bloodshed, murder, robbery, and pillage of the Thirty Years War raged until 1648. Even after the end of the war, discrimination and maltreatment lingered for more than a century. Motivated by fear and a desire to worship God freely, German Protestants eventually fled.

England's Queen Anne sympathized and financed the voyages of those desiring a new life in America. An English ship, *America*, brought the first recorded German immigrants (as well as immigrants from other nations) to Philadelphia on August 20, 1683. They eagerly anticipated a new life, free from persecution. Unfortunately, the harsh conditions facing the colonists exacted a high price for the precious freedom they sought.

As a young university student, William Penn associated with religious radicals. Because of this association and his extreme ideas, Oxford expelled the son of the prominent English family. Deeply disappointed, Admiral Sir William Penn sent his son to Ireland in an attempt to distance him from the extremist group. In Ireland, the young man met and joined the Quakers, the most radical and persecuted of all the Protestant sects. Persecution and later imprisonment drove them to seek freedom in the New World.

In 1682, at the age of thirty-eight, William Penn sailed to America on the ship, *Welcome*, and established a colony on American land. He used his family's wealth and influence and acquired land grants as payment of a debt owed to his father by King Charles II. Initially, settlers referred to the new colony as Penn's Woods. The young leader preferred Sylvania, a Latin word meaning forest. King Charles called the land *Penn's Sylvania* to honor the family name. Pennsylvania embodied the pioneers' determination to worship freely; some called it a holy experiment – a colony dedicated to religious tolerance.

Penn traveled to Germany and encouraged Protestants to join him in the new colony. Perhaps because of his mother's German heritage, his strong dedication to religious freedom, or both, he extended the invitation. He spoke of the beauty of the Poconos and Alleghenies, and beckoned oppressed groups with assurances of similarities between Pennsylvania and Germany.

His mission succeeded. The compelling promise of freedom motivated demoralized peasants. They willingly exchanged reality of a known hell on earth for the potential hell of the voyage and wilderness. A small band of Quakers and Mennonites founded Germantown, Pennsylvania in 1683. Other persecuted groups including the Amish, Dunkers, Moravians, Schwenfelders, and Probsts followed. Farmers, craftsmen, artisans, homemakers, doctors, and lawyers – German, French, and Swiss Protestant embarked on the journey – a journey to freedom.

The voyage to America proved costly and long. Passengers from Rotterdam to Philadelphia paid five to ten pounds of sterling, a great sum for those days. Children traveled for half-price, though few under the age of seven survived the voyage. Crossing the Atlantic took eight to sixteen weeks, and the immigrants endured deplorable conditions. Crews rarely planned enough food or supplies for the entire trip. Storms claimed many vessels. Typhus, dysentery, smallpox, scurvy, and other diseases ravaged the travelers. Commonly, starvation and death occurred before the ship reached its destination.

If the voyagers survived ocean passage, they faced additional scrutiny upon arrival. Once the ship docked, a doctor boarded and examined the surviving passengers. Those who showed no indication of illness disembarked and continued to the colony, but the authorities turned away anyone showing signs of illness. Sick passengers remained on the ship. If they survived the return voyage, they returned to Europe.

Reaching Philadelphia failed to guarantee good fortune. Most ships arrived in the fall, with a harsh winter ahead. Though many succumbed, others faced the hardships, survived, and experienced the freedom for which they risked their lives. Germans earned a reputation of being obstinate – a character trait that sustained them in the struggle against their homeland rulers, the voyage to America, the wilderness, and the Indians. Despite difficulties, new settlers continued to come to the colonies.

While most Germans fled to America seeking religious freedom, the Irish sought relief from extreme poverty. During America's infancy, almost half of the population of Ireland lived on farms that produced little income. Because most Irish people depended on potatoes for food, three successive years of failed potato crops led to a great famine with dire consequences. Over seventy thousand people died of starvation. Desperate for a better life, two million Irish eventually relocated to America.

Many Europeans who lacked funds essentially sold themselves as payment. Indentured servants agreed to work for their master for three to seven years in exchange for passage to America. Most made the trip willingly, though unscrupulous merchants tricked others into service. In order to pay their fares, many parents got off the ship and sold their children like cattle. The children served until they reached the age of twenty-one. At the end of the term, servants might receive clothes, tools, a small sum of money, or even a piece of land. An estimated fifty to seventy-five percent of white American colonists paid for passage to America by selling themselves or their children.

Unable to purchase land and establish rural homesteads, the Irish congregated in the cities where they landed and worked at any job they found. In contrast to impoverished Irish immigrants, many Germans arrived in America with enough money to purchase property. Instead of gathering in crowded cities seeking work, they chose to journey further west in search of successful land ownership.

Anti-immigration sentiment invaded the culture during the Industrial Revolution. The vast numbers of German and Irish immigrants resulted in an eruption of hostility and violent outbursts. Opposition grew from religious and political differences.

The largest ethnic and anti-Catholic riot occurred in Philadelphia in 1844. Protestants, Catholics and local militia fought in the streets. Sixteen people died, dozens sustained injuries, and the crowds destroyed over forty buildings.

Political opposition rose from needs created by the economic depression of the time. Immigrants living in the cities joined the Democrats, because the party focused on issues of the common people. Americans in low-paying jobs felt threatened. Often foreign workers willing to work for almost nothing in order to survive replaced American workers. Signs that read NINA – "No Irish Need Apply" – sprang up throughout the country.

Nativist political parties sprang up overnight. The most influential, The Know Nothings, supported a platform of anti-Catholic rhetoric and lobbied to extend the amount of time it took immigrants to become citizens and voters. They also tried to prevent foreign-born people from ever holding public office.

1889 cartoon stereotypes the Irish as unmixable in the American melting pot

Economic recovery after the 1844 depression reduced serious confrontations for a time, but the fragile truce collapsed as nativism resurged. In 1856, American Party presidential candidate, Millard Filmore, trumpeted anti-immigration themes. The political landscape splintered. Republicans, with no position on immigration, benefitted and rode to a victory in the divisive election of 1860.

During the middle half of the nineteenth century, more than half the population of Ireland immigrated to the United States. An equal number of Germans joined their countrymen, who braved the wilderness more than a century earlier. Most fled their homeland because of civil unrest, severe unemployment, and unbearable conditions at home. This wave brought more than seven and a half million immigrants to the United States – more than the entire population of the country in 1810. Nearly all came from northern and western Europe – about a third from Ireland and another third from Germany. Growing American companies absorbed all who wanted work.

Immigrants built canals, constructed railroads, and engaged in labor-intensive endeavors.

The family tree provides clues to the daily life of our ancestors. Most census records list occupations of farmer, or housework with the required work ethic implied. Church records document a strong connection to the local Baptist Church with a significant number of Baptist ministers in the family.

Often small communities resent new people changing the neighborhood. We settle into a comfort zone and react to anything that threatens our way of life. What we experience on a small scale, society magnifies. Only American Indians legitimately claim native status. At some point, someone in every family immigrated to America.

A native Texan, I proudly call Texas my home. I've never lived, nor do I want to live anywhere else. I welcome friends and neighbors from other states and other countries. They enrich my life. I learn from them. They make me a better person.

I claim to bleed red, white, and blue. While curiosity prompts me to consider DNA testing, I suspect it would prove what I already know. I am a product of the American melting pot – Luck of the Irish – Obstinate nature of the German – Abiding faith of the German Baptists - Dignity of the English – Yankee ingenuity – Texas proud.

Where in the World is Noodle, Texas, and How in the World Did We Get Here?

"Land is the only thing in the world
that amounts to anything."
Margaret Mitchell, from Gone with the Wind

Residents of villages throughout Germany positioned themselves closer to the speaker, eager to hear the claims in the latest installment of letters from Fredrich Diercks in America, now better known by his Texas alias, Johann Fredrich Ernst. Other ambitious leaders perceived immigration as a solution to the economic, social, political, and religious problems of the homeland. Using his forceful personality, Ernst encouraged young families to follow him to Texas.

A professional gardener, Ernst intended to settle in Missouri but a land grant of 4000 acres enticed him to form a German settlement near Austin, Texas. He influenced prospective settlers by writing lengthy accounts to friends in Germany. He described a land with an abundant supply of fish and game. Procuring the food source required no license. Fertile land with a winterless climate awaited German skills and labor to produce an abundant harvest. Immigrants claimed land for only a surveyor's fee and paid minimal taxes. Persuasive reports depicted a Texas paradise, downplaying or omitting any negative aspects.

Throughout his life in Germany, Fredrick Deutschman listened to stories of life in America. As a teenager, Fredrick (Fritz) Deutschman, emigrated from Germany to the United States. Census records document his arrival in 1872 at the age of nineteen. Like many German immigrants, Fritz farmed the land. By the age of twenty-six, he found his way to McLellan County, Texas where he met and married Texas native, Sarah Raney. The young German supported his family by farming the land near Waco. At the turn of the twentieth century, the young family included two sons and a daughter, Sarah's widowed mother and a young nephew, Benjamin Dunn. His pioneer spirit drove him to work hard and save money. Finally, he possessed enough cash to purchase his own land.

Even seasoned Texas travelers fail to recognize Noodle. Only people with a personal connection to the community assign any importance to its origins. The Noodle/Horn Community took its name from Noodle Creek. According to folk tradition, the name was derived from an Indian word defined as *nothing* or *signifying a dry creek bed.*

In 1882, Anderson Criswell, a shepherd, settled in the area. The following year settlers built the first school on Mr. Criswell's land. Settlers came for affordable land priced at $5 per acre. By 1898, a store opened to serve the community. By 1920, land prices doubled and the town supported a gin, a blacksmith shop, and a garage. The Noodle post office operated from 1900 to 1924. The progressive and industrious inhabitants of the black farmland bordering the

Clear Fork of the Brazos River distinguished themselves as successful farmers.

Eager to work his own land, Fritz seized the opportunity to establish a homestead and brought his family to the small west Texas community. By the time the young family arrived in 1901, land prices doubled. Sarah and Fritz purchased one hundred eight acres in the Noodle/Horn Community for $1085. A shrewd businessman, Fritz, explored every opportunity to add properties to his estate. The couple established themselves as vital members of the community. Fritz and Sarah joined the R. R. Horn, Edgar Boaz, D. C. Herring, and John Womack families as the earliest settlers of the area.

Community life revolved around school and church. Early settlers established a school on the Criswell Ranch. When the first school ceased to exist, the community contracted Mary Barley of Commerce to teach in a one-room, twenty by forty foot box house on the Boaz Ranch. Thirty students attended. Over the next four years, the population increased and Mr. Herring deeded four acres for educational purposes. The Horn District opened in 1910 and consisted of one building containing two classrooms. The school educated Noodle's children until the district consolidated to form Noodle-Horn in 1935.

The Baptist congregation at Horn formed in 1911 and initially met in the new schoolhouse. The first pastor, a Mr. Robinett from Union, organized the church. The community celebrated the dedication of a new building, Amity Baptist Church, also on Horn land, in 1924. One source lists Sarah Deutschman as a charter member of the church. An oil well on the church property provided financial support for the church and school for several years.

The Deutschman heirs established their own families. Both Fredrick Benjamin and C.L. purchased land from their father. Their sister lived in a nearby community with her husband. The 1919 land deed documents a land purchase of 75 acres. F. B. Deutschman and Verna (named only as wife in the legal document) paid $1500 cash to his father.

Each discovery raises more questions. The young couple struggled financially. So, where did the young Fred and Verna get $1500 cash? Fred's death in 1928 left his young widow destitute. His obituary mentioned nothing about his parents.

What happened to Fritz and Sarah? Jones County records reveal the sale of land liens to C.L. in 1924. The land deed lists the couple as sellers. However, no additional documents bear their names after that date – no death certificates or burial records.

Fast forward to Sunday afternoon, January 2016 – My sister and I set out to explore the mystery. With the help of GPS, we easily found the Shiloh Cemetery just west of Noodle. In the center of the cemetery, we located the family plot. A tall headstone stands in the center, and documents the life and death of Fredrick Benjamin Deutschman. Interestingly the name on the gravestone is misspelled. Following a lead from another family member, we identified the graves of Sarah and Fritz. Unfortunately, the metal markers are illegible – no names – no dates – no clues – new discoveries – more questions. Why did the son have an impressive memorial, while the parents remain unmarked? Who paid for the monument?

Our family connection to Noodle, Texas begins here. Fritz and Sarah purchased and worked the land. They established roots. He sold land to his son, Fred, and daughter-in-law, Verna Deutschman. The young widow remarried. John and Verna Carr worked the land and raised a blended family. This inheritance tied our family to the land of my childhood memories.

The Band of Hope

Story of band of cattle and horse rustlers known as the Noodle gang
Author Unknown

West Texas Historical Association Year Book Volume XXI
October 1945 pp 79-80

There is a wailing over in the land of Noodle
Where there was once lots of cows and boodle,
They ring their hands in deep despair
For Tyson and his deputies have been there.

When the gay and festive Jimmie Camp,
Who held a lot a burning lamp,
The grand jury saw how the work was done
And that explains how the fight begun.

For fifteen times did they indict
The names of those written at night;
And after taking the usual vote,
The indictments were returned into open court.

They scrambled a while in the clough of despond,
Then they took on new life and rustled for bond.
While Breedlove his great big knife,
And calculated how to pin them for life.

Fred Cockrell, Word, and Woodruff swore,
Christenberry spoke until his throat was sore.
Grundy Thurmond came on like a thousand of brick,
While the jury sat still and caught on the trick.

Cunningham prances while Hamner pawd air.
Dick Davis was camping right close to the lair.
While Breedlove stood around as if free from care,
But the jury could see he was loaded for bear.

The juries were composed of twelve good men,
And they generally said, "Three years in the pen."
While defendants looked bad off of their range,
For them liberty to confinement is an awful change.

And there is weeping now for Noodle's sons,
And wailing now where the streamlet runs,
And the old cow looks on with gladsome smile,
Thinking she is safe for a little while.

High-heeled boots for convict stripes;
Close cut hair and penitentiary pipes;
They have laid aside their jingling spurs,
And are watched and guarded until their release occurs.

Here is a prayer for your repentance boys,
When far removed from pleasant joys,
May you resolve when again set free,
To turn aside from the tempter's plea.

Learn your lesson and learn it well
Think of life before you fell,
And when released from the gruesome pen,
Resolve forthwith to be honest men.

TYLER

Anglo Saxon, English, French
Meaning of the surname Tyler –
Occupational surname for a maker
or layer of tiles. In the Middle Ages
tiles were widely used in floors and
pavements, and to a lesser extent in
roofing, where they did not really
come into their own until the 16th
century.

Coker

Olde English, Midieval
Meaning of the surname Coker –
Warrior, fighter
Alternative meaning – builder of hay
ricks or stacks

William
Hodges
1815 – 1867

Sarah
Ann
Shipp
1827 –1897

William
Coker
1837 – 1900

Amanda
Christian
Hodges
1853 – 1900

William S.
Tyler
1873 – ?

Sarah Jemima
Caldonia
Coker
1873 –1939

Mary
Verna
Tyler
1895 – 1984

The Saga Begins
Verna and Fred

*"You don't develop courage by being happy in your relationships
every day. You develop it by surviving difficult times and
challenging adversity."*
Epicurus

"I had to borrow money to buy appropriate shoes and clothing for my children to wear to their father's funeral," Granny shared.

I sat quietly listening to my grandmother share the story of her life as a young widow. She spoke frankly with no more emotion than she attached to discussing the dinner menu. Years later I realized she never shared with any of her four daughters the information she revealed to me on a hot summer afternoon. She continued with stories, leaving little doubt about the troubled nature of her first marriage. Fred Benjamin Deutschman failed to be the ideal husband and father she desired. She described a hard drinking husband who worked sporadically and failed to provide for his young family.

The family legend reported Fred's death as a tragic farming accident. The Abilene Reporter News, February 22, 1928 described a far different account of the young man's demise than the veiled references of the family account. Rather than a tragic accidental death under an overturned farm tractor, the newspaper revealed a more sinister incident. "C. L. Deutschman of Abilene was advised yesterday of the death of his brother, Fred B. Deutschman at Ranger, Tuesday morning at 6:32. Death resulted from injuries received a week ago. Fred Deutschman was employed by the Lone Star Gas Company and was run down and crushed by a company tractor, two miles from Ranger. His chest was crushed, several ribs were broken, and internal injuries were received."

The obituary listed by name his brother, C. L. Deutschman, and his sister, Mrs. O.R. Byrd as survivors. The paper listed his wife as Berna Tyler, with three unnamed children. The misspelling of the widow's name and the omission of the children's names hints at a rift in the extended family.

The reference to Fred being "run down and crushed" by a co-worker reveals something about his character. Was he drinking? Did he enrage the wrong co-worker? What really happened? Accident or murder – regardless – a tragic end to a young man's life.

What did I do to deserve this life? How did I wind up in this mess? How will I ever care for three children? The young widow agonized as she reflected on the decisions leading to this point in her life.

Verna Mary Tyler's life began in Tyler, Texas. After her father abandoned the family, her mother remarried James Kirby. The family moved frequently. She met Fred Deutschman near Waco. He represented the ticket to the secure married life of her dreams. Unfortunately, their life took some unexpected turns.

The Deutschman patriarch, Fritz, purchased land in the West Texas community of Noodle. Fred, his brother, and sister followed their father with visions of a better life.

Sadly, her dream of a tranquil family life soon turned into a nightmare. Granny shared little of the details of her life with Fred. She spoke tersely of a lack of financial resources and a mean-tempered spouse. Fred drank heavily and spent much of what he earned on alcohol. Every man in her life disappointed her, an absent father, a cruel stepfather, and now a bad marriage.

Verna never considered divorce. When Will Tyler abandoned the family, she suffered the loss of her father's love. Even if it meant sacrificing herself, she determined her children would know their father. She resigned herself to the only life she knew. Perhaps she prayed for God to change her husband. If Fred failed to change, she prayed for strength to endure.

Often she wondered *how much worse can things get.* Verna soon learned. When Fred died, things got even more difficult.

In 1920s Texas, women expected to marry, bear children, and make a home for the family. Very few women worked outside the home. Verna never visualized herself in this situation. February 1928, the thirty-year old young mother found herself without money or assets with two young daughters and an infant son dependent on her.

Desperate and alone, without resources, she took inventory of her talents and skills. She knew how to cook and clean, and she possessed excellent skills as a seamstress. For the next two years, she capitalized on her abilities and supported her little family by washing, ironing and making clothes for members of the community.

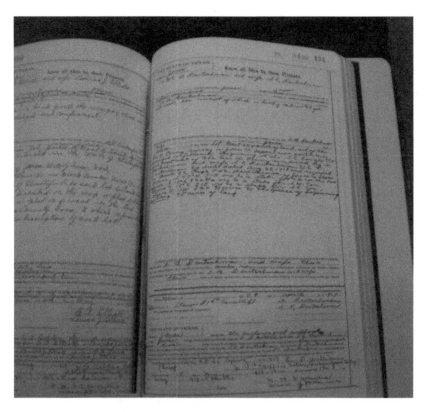

**Jones County Deed Record documenting the sale of land to
Fred B. Deutschman and wife**

CARR

Celtic, Norse, Scottish, English
Meaning of the surname Carr –
Fighter, warrior, battle
Alternate meanings and origins of the
surname Carr – Variant of the surname
Kerr of Northern England and Scottish
– meaning topographical name of
someone who lived near a patch of wet
ground overgrown with brush
Irish meaning – Anglicized form of
Gaelic meaning spear
Alternate Irish of Gaelic meaning –
warrior, fighter, battle

Jacobs

Origin – Biblical, American, Hebrew
Meaning of the surname Jacobs –
Supplanter, one who undermines, heel

41

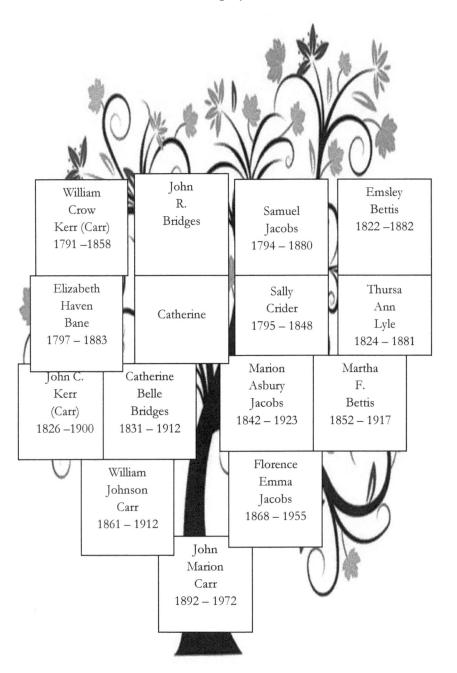

William Crow Kerr (Carr) 1791 –1858

John R. Bridges

Samuel Jacobs 1794 – 1880

Emsley Bettis 1822 –1882

Elizabeth Haven Bane 1797 – 1883

Catherine

Sally Crider 1795 – 1848

Thursa Ann Lyle 1824 – 1881

John C. Kerr (Carr) 1826 –1900

Catherine Belle Bridges 1831 – 1912

Marion Asbury Jacobs 1842 – 1923

Martha F. Bettis 1852 – 1917

William Johnson Carr 1861 – 1912

Florence Emma Jacobs 1868 – 1955

John Marion Carr 1892 – 1972

A Family of Gentle Giants

"John Carr lived on the old France Polly place. He cared for the sick, broke wild stock, and did more work than any man in the community. He was a giant of a man who didn't know his own strength."
Merkel Area History

"I drove a horse drawn milk wagon from Rockwall through Dallas to Oak Cliff, Texas. I'd leave before dawn and return home after dark," Granddaddy Carr responded when I brought my fiancée to meet him and told him about our plans to live in Oak Cliff after our June wedding.

Oak Cliff of Granddaddy's youth contrasted sharply with my new neighborhood. In the late nineteenth century, Oak Cliff boasted a thriving economy and proudly served as a vacation and resort destination. The bustling community supported four grocery stores, two meat markets, a hardware store, and a feed store. Granddaddy delivered fresh milk from the family's Rockwall farm to the stores on Jefferson Blvd.

"The people in Oak Cliff didn't want to be a part of Dallas. Proud to be their own city, the successful business owners bragged about beautiful houses on tree lined streets. The leaders of Dallas kept trying until they finally swallowed up the smaller town," he reminisced about turn of the century events.

My description of the 1969 neighborhood sharply contrasted with Granddaddy's memories of an area he abandoned more than sixty years earlier. A few sections of brick pavement remained on Jefferson Street and hinted at the city's history. Nothing else even vaguely resembled the landscape he remembered. Sears department store provided the hub of local business. Several restaurants offered affordable dining experiences. Beauty salons and barbershops served the citizens. Local banks provided financial services to the community.

Though the Texas Theater struggled to survive, its status as a significant historic site prevented demolition. The theater earned the infamous designation when Lee Harvey Oswald hid in the theater after shooting President John F. Kennedy. A local merchant, John Brewer, recognized Oswald and alerted theater employee, Julia Postal, who called police. Fifteen officers converged on the theater and arrested Oswald.

The one common link of the early and mid twentieth century community – Jefferson Boulevard remained the center of commerce and a recognizable landmark – the main street of Oak Cliff, Texas.

"I like your young man," with those few words, my grandfather gave his approval of my marriage.

A physically imposing man, Granddaddy commanded respect. He raised his children with a strong moral compass and strictly enforced discipline. However, grandchildren experienced his softer, gentler side. He never physically disciplined me. I rarely heard him raise his voice in anger. A simple disapproving look made further discipline unnecessary.

He wore a pair of overalls every day. Getting dressed up meant a clean shirt and freshly laundered overalls.

Whether he headed to the field or to town, each time he left the house he donned a brimmed leather hat. When he smiled, the dimples in his cheeks and the twinkle in his blue eyes suggested some mischievous scheme.

John Marion Carr entered the world in Scranton, Texas on March 8, 1892. His mother named him to honor his maternal grandfather Marion Asbury Jacobs. The Carr/Jacob's ancestral roots include a melting pot of European immigrants. Ancestors left England, Scotland, Norway, and Germany to seek opportunity in the United States as early as the mid sixteen hundreds. Settling initially in Pennsylvania and Virginia, they migrated southward through Tennessee and by the early 1900's most of the family lived in Texas.

A nineteen-year-old Florence Emma Jacobs married William Johnson Carr in Tennessee. One year later, she delivered her first son, Carl Harvey. The young family soon moved to Texas where they lived the remainder of their lives, first in Rising Star and later in Rockwall County. Twenty-two years after the birth of her first child, she gave birth to her youngest son, Henry Alvin. Over twenty-two years the couple welcomed a total of nine sons and two daughters. One of the children, George Grady, died in infancy. Another son, William Farley, suffered a ruptured appendix and died as a young adult.

When her husband, William, died the year following Henry's birth, Florence raised her younger children alone in Rockwall County. Fifteen years later, she married Thomas Orr, who died only three years after their marriage. As the grandchildren arrived, she assumed the role of family matriarch and the title, Granny Orr.

Her strong faith affected every aspect of her life. Granny Orr's obituary in the Clifton Record newspaper, December 9, 1955, emphasized the importance of faith, friends, and family, "At the age of 13 years, Mrs. Orr was baptized in Tennessee as a member of the Baptist Church. She remained an active and faithful member of this denomination throughout the rest of her lifetime wherever she lived. Upon moving to Clifton, she affiliated with the First Baptist Church and as long as she was physically able, she attended every worship service and every related activity at this local church. It could be said that Mrs. Orr throughout the years divided her time and energies equally between the needs of her family and those of her church and its members. The two – her family and her church – were her life. Her pleasing affable personality made many friends for her everywhere."

By the early 1950s, the Carr siblings pursued active lives. Early years trained the brothers to farm the land and served to build the muscles of the naturally strong men. Though seven of the remaining siblings lived in Texas, family gatherings occurred rarely as they lived more than a four-hour drive apart. However, when family members assembled, their commanding size, strong personalities, and authoritarian voices impressed and intimidated the younger generation.

The second oldest son, John, lived most of his life in West Texas and established a reputation in the Noodle, Texas community as a strong, hard working young man. He married Mary, the daughter of the well-respected Benningfield family. A little older than average newlyweds of the day, they wanted children and soon after their marriage two sons, Murrell and Grady, blessed their family. However, life changed drastically when his wife became ill and died of acute appendicitis. At thirty-two, John found himself unprepared to care for his two infant sons. He relied on his in-laws to help with the children, while he worked hard to provide as a single father. He and the Benningfield family remained close even after he remarried.

Six years after Mary's death, he married the young widow, Verna Deutschman, a marriage lasting over forty-two years. The blended family consisted of his two sons, her two daughters and one son, and soon their two daughters.

Most of the Carr brothers spent some time working as farmers. However, several brothers eventually abandoned the farm and sought other careers. The eldest son, Carl, pastored several West Texas Baptist congregations. The family trait for booming voices served the preacher well. Frank often sang in the Merkel church, and his legendary bass never required a microphone. The two youngest sons made their homes in Clifton, Texas. Henry pursued a career with Lone Star Gas. Elected as Sheriff of Bosque County in 1960, Audrey served two terms.

Thunderous voices matched the daunting physical appearance of each member of the Carr clan. When one or more family members gathered, the room filled with conversation at an escalating volume as each family member talked over the other.

The unusual quiet indicated the serious purpose for our rare automobile trip. Granddaddy rode in the passenger seat, solemn faced. None of the normal chatter broke the silence during the four-hour drive from Noodle to Clifton, Texas. He focused on memories of his brother, and none of us dared interrupt his thoughts. We stopped to ask directions, but the task proved to be more difficult than anyone imagined. Every downtown business closed for the day. *It's not a holiday. I wonder where everyone is.* I thought.

The sign on the door of a local business explained. "Closed in memory and honor of Henry Carr."

Everyone in Clifton knew and loved the Carr family. The youngest Carr brother managed the local natural gas company and served as a deacon in the local Baptist church. His death shocked the family as well as the small community. Diagnosed with metastatic lung cancer, he declined rapidly and died two months later.

After the funeral, the family congregated at Henry's home. I quietly observed family members. The physical presence of my grandfather, his brothers, and sisters awed smaller, younger family members. Uncle Audrey dwarfed his older brother, my granddaddy. Being separated by time and distance failed to diminish the family bond. Apart from their imposing physical presence, their personal commitment to honesty, integrity, and service to others produced strength of character.

My grandfather, John, developed skills as a farmer and rancher. His neighbors relied on his physical strength when they needed help. The community counted on his honesty, integrity, and wise counsel. Neighbors depended on his tender side to care for the sick. He exemplified the guiding principles learned from his mother – family, faith, and service to the community.

The Old Country Church

"Church attendance is as vital to a disciple as a transfusion of rich, healthy blood to a sick man."
Dwight L. Moody

Social life of the Noodle/Horn Community revolved around church. Initially, the local church met in a one-room schoolhouse. The original settlers of this area placed importance on the spiritual development of their children. Old minutes document the organization of the Amity Baptist Church on October 8, 1911. Mrs. R. R. Horn, Mr. and Mrs. J. N. Hatfield, and Sarah Deutschman (mother-in-law of Granny Carr) served as charter members. The church thrived as more families arrived and settled on the surrounding farms. Christians of all denominations attended the local church. The congregation raised money to erect a church building and celebrated the dedication on June 8, 1924. Mrs. Nan Horn donated the land for the church. Mary Eno Mundell recalled her grandmother's words, "Your grandfather gave the land for the educational welfare of the children. I'm giving it for their spiritual welfare." (Merkel Area History p. 46)

Amity Church exerted a strong influence on the faith and character of the Carr and Dooly families. One former pastor shared a story of Granddaddy Carr, who literally knocked the church off its foundation. Perhaps distracted or maybe just in a rush to get home to Sunday dinner, Granddaddy put his truck in reverse and backed into the corner of the church building. Fortunately, he stopped before completely shoving the frame building off the concrete foundation blocks. His mishap provided the source of joking and perhaps inspiration for more than one of the young minister's sermons.

"Would you like to meet William Thorne?" Aunt Mary Bailey asked after we finished lunch.

"I'd love to meet Dr. Thorne. I've heard and read much about him. I'd really like to hear his stories about the Amity Church and my grandparents." I replied.

We drove across the campus of the Baptist Retirement Village in San Angelo, Texas, where Dr. Thorne visited with other residents of the village. Aunt Mary waited patiently for a break in the conversation before she introduced me to the distinguished gentleman, "Dr. Thorne this is John Carr's granddaughter."

My name never registered with the elderly retired minister, but my grandfather's name obviously triggered a flood of memories. He smiled broadly and repeated my grandfather's name. "John Carr" he paused as if visualizing the face of his old friend.

"John Carr was the salt of the earth, and that little church was my very first congregation. John Carr – It's been a long time since I thought of him. I have many fond memories of the people of the Amity Church. I was a city slicker from Houston, a broke student at Hardin Simmons College, unaccustomed to rural traditions. That little congregation taught me how to be a pastor."

I listened as Dr. Thorne spoke of the small rural congregation. "They took care of me. Your grandfather made sure someone took me home for lunch every Sunday. The church debated how much they should pay me. One farmer felt they shouldn't consider such an exorbitant salary, as he'd never heard a sermon worth $7. They debated for what seemed like an eternity, while I waited outside in the yard. One deacon came outside and told me it was looking good. I guess they must have been pleased with the job I did, because after a few years they increased my pay to $10 a week."

He continued with another example of the rural church's generosity. "During that time, I became ill and had to be hospitalized. I never saw a bill from the hospital. The farmers of the community took up a collection to cover the cost. During very lean times, church members sacrificed from their meager resources to provide for my physical needs and pay my medical bills. They were good people."

When the Horn school consolidated with Noodle, church attendance declined. Though a lease with the Idaho Oil and Gas Company provided royalties and a much-needed influx of cash, the congregation struggled to meet obligations. By 1953, the church no longer held services at Amity. The building stood empty for many years. Granddaddy Carr continued to serve as a deacon. Joined by a few remaining trustees, he took care of the building and furnishings. By 1970, they liquidated all assets.

As the Amity Church declined, most of the members united with nearby Noodle Baptist. Organized in 1924, Noodle Baptist Church met about six miles south of the Amity location. By 1950, church members owned cars allowing the freedom to travel to the growing congregation.

The committed group of Christians determined to serve God, care for each other, and provide a spiritual foundation for their children. They erected an old, box style church at the Crossroads across from Noodle School. Twenty years later the church building leaned to the south and looked as if it might collapse at any time.

The church set aside money for a new building. Finances required church members to provide manual labor for construction of the church structure. They procrastinated until one summer afternoon in 1946; a group of church members led by Vertice Eller took action. He found a group of men visiting at the Noodle Store. Mr. Eller organized a work crew who carried the piano and the pews out of the church and placed them under the tabernacle. A couple of cars pulled the building over. A bonfire completed the demolition. Members of the church volunteered their various skills to build the church and held their first service in the new building in December 1947.

The Amity and Noodle churches provided spiritual education for the rural residents. The families of the community gathered to share their joys and sorrows. Their shared faith bonded them together. Like many of the family farmhouses, the Amity Church building no longer stands. Noodle Baptist Church continues to welcome worshipers in the twenty-first century.

Gathering at the Amity Baptist Church – Includes family members from extended Carr, Dooly, and Williams families.

Disgusting Habit

"Nothing so needs reforming as other people's habits. "
Mark Twain

"I loved those salt-of-the-earth folks in Noodle. They took good care of their preacher," recalled the elderly minister of his first pastorate at the Amity Baptist Church located in the Noodle/Horn Community. "But they *did* love to dip snuff. After an animated conversation with one of them, you felt the need to go wash your face."

"My Granny and Granddaddy Carr really did enjoy dipping snuff," I agreed.

The practice evolved from the use of dry snuff in early American history. Its use grew more popular in the rural south than in large cities. In the early nineteenth century, growers produced a powdered form of tobacco, which customers sniffed nasally. Americans found an oral use by chewing the end of a twig until it resembled a brush. Then they "dipped" the twig in the snuff and placed it in their mouths until the tobacco dissolved. Copenhagen introduced moist snuff in 1822. Skoal first produced my grandparent's preferred brand in 1934.

The typical tobacco user employed a routine, using the thumb and middle finger to flick snuff into the lid of the can. Then the index finger picked up the damp, brown powder and placed it between the lower lip and gum.

The natural cause-effect of oral tobacco created excess saliva. If outdoors, men usually spit the excess tobacco-filled fluid on the ground. A lady refrained "dipping" until she found an available spit-can. Granny strategically placed containers around the house to collect the brown byproduct. The brass urn-shaped spittoon belonged to Granddaddy, and no one else dared touch it. Granny picked it up only to empty and clean it. For her personal use, she preferred a recycled aluminum can.

Tell-tell signs of chew collected around the corners of the snuff user's mouth and warned visitors of the potential hazard. A wise person maintained a safe distance when engaging the "dipper" in conversation. Otherwise, spatter likely found its way onto the clothes or worse, the skin, of the visitor.

The youthful Houston born minister, Bill Thorne, quickly learned the rural customs of his first congregation. He discovered how to avoid the chewing tobacco spray by positioning himself to the side or at a safe distance from the dipper. A solution for the Lord's Supper common cup proved more problematic. During the first observance of the ordinance with his new congregation, he identified a significant problem. The congregation partook of the common loaf. No problem. As the loaf passed from person to person, each worshipper pinched off a piece of bread until each person received the sacrament.

The cup presented a different challenge. As it passed from member to member, each sipped from the large silver cup. As he observed the congregation with tobacco stained mouths, every eye gazed expectantly at him. Nothing in his limited experience prepared him for this moment. *I can do this. Before the next observation, I'll find a solution.*

He received the cup from the deacon and took a deep breath. Ignoring the tobacco stains on the rim of the cup, he blessed the cup and drank the juice symbolizing Christ's blood.

Driving home Sunday evening, he determined to find a way to avoid tobacco juice in any of its various forms. His obsession with shared snuff motivated the naïve young pastor to spend a portion of his limited income to purchase individual communion cups complete with a silver-plated serving tray. He proudly presented the gift to the parishioners. Their lack of enthusiasm surprised him. "We've always used the common cup. Brother D, a charter member of the church, donated the silver cup in memory of his late wife. The silversmith engraved it with a special inscription. Some of the people won't like it, but we'll try the little cups this time."

By the next quarter, the new communion cups disappeared. No one remembered which member offered to wash the little glasses. The silver cup occupied its usual place beside the common loaf of bread. The minister, a little older and much wiser, modified the worship order. He incorporated the importance of the elements in his sermon before serving the bread and grape juice. When he served the congregation, he took his portion before passing the elements to the rest of the congregation.

Thinking Outside the Box

"To repurpose a thought, idea, or memory to a new purpose is the height of creativity."
Steve Supple

I pulled the box down from the top of Mom's closet and carried it to the living room where she supervised packing from her recliner. "What's this?" I asked as I flipped the simple latch and revealed sheet music and songbooks.

"Granddaddy made that for Granny to use as suitcase."

A few words immediately transformed the simple wooden crate to a treasured heirloom created by the strong but loving hands of my grandfather. My grandparents lived frugally and pleasure travel represented an unattainable luxury. The farm animals required constant care. While neighbors willingly pitched in when a family experienced an emergency, they rarely asked each other for help. My grandfather understood how hard each farmer worked and declined to burden them with additional chores.

The purpose for Granny's travel remains a mystery. Perhaps she traveled to care for an ailing relative or attend the funeral of a close relation. Early in the twentieth century, most people traveled by train. After World War I, (from 1930 – 1950) the bus became the preferred method of travel. Those who could afford automobiles drove themselves causing the railroads to lose business. Granny never drove the family car. If a situation required a woman to travel without her husband, she chose between two travel options. The train presented the more luxurious method. However, most farm wives chose the more affordable fare of a Greyhound bus.

Mother recalled Christmas socks filled with an orange and perhaps a peppermint stick. The family enjoyed peaches, plums, and wild berries grown on the farm. Grown and packaged in California, oranges provided a rare treat for the west Texas farm family. Prior to World War II, citrus fruit growers packaged produce in wooden crates. The delivery containing 10 pounds of oranges arrived in a box measuring slightly less than ten by sixteen inches. After the family consumed the oranges, granddaddy saved the crate and utilized it as a storage container.

Verna and John Carr

When Granny needed a suitcase, he retrieved the wooden crate. He attached hinges and a metal handle. A simple latch, made from a screen-door hook, served to close and secure the contents. An emblem stamped directly into the wood pictured a golden sunrise. Over the years, the name of the produce company faded. Only "grown and packed in California" remained legible. By the early fifties, cardboard boxes replaced the more expensive, substantial wooden crates.

The wooden shipping containers, advertised as vintage items on modern internet websites, command much more than the original monetary cost.

As Granny boarded the bus to attend to some urgent need, she proudly carried her little case, lovingly designed by the hands of her husband. Though I rarely saw open displays of affection between my grandparents, I never questioned their love for and commitment to each other. The value of a little rectangular shipping crate repurposed to a suitcase – minimal. The love it represents – Priceless!

The Value of Play

"Men do not quit playing because they grow old; they grow old because they quit playing."
Oliver Wendall Holmes

The afternoon presented the perfect opportunity for one-on-one time with my mom. I visited her apartment with the intentional goal of extracting some of her memories. I prompted. "Tell me your favorite childhood memory."

She sat quietly contemplating the question before she finally replied, "I remember playing house with Mary John under a big tree in front of the farmhouse."

My mother's birth occurred in the middle of the Great Depression. The farm provided enough produce, eggs, milk, and meat to feed the large family. Scarce cash provided necessities like shoes, material for clothing, and seeds for the next season's crops. Living frugally allowed enough to survive but left little for luxuries. Money spent for toys represented a waste of precious resources. The children learned to create their own playthings. Each girl possessed one treasured doll.

Mom continued, "Before school each year, Daddy would sell either a calf or a hog. Each of the children got a new pair of shoes to start the new school year. Christmas usually meant we got an orange, some nuts and a peppermint stick in our sock. One Christmas was different. We were so excited when we received a special gift."

"I really wanted a set of dishes to play house." Tears escaped Mom's eyes as she recalled a treasured Christmas gift. "Daddy made us a set of dishes. He saved tin cans and their lids and created dishes for us."

I imagined my granddaddy using creative ingenuity to construct a special gift for his daughters. After a long day in the field, he waited until the girls slept. He took tin snips and pliers and carefully bent the sharp edges of the tin lids to create plates and the tin cups to serve as glasses. He crimped the sharp edges to avoid any cut or injury to the little girls. On Christmas morning, the children squealed with delight. They clutched their dolls and ran into the yard, where they prepared and served a pretend Christmas feast.

My thoughts flashed back to times spent at the farm. Granny gathered cast off clothes, plastic butter dishes, and unused utensils. The old washhouse provided our playhouse. We baked mud pies, and created concoctions using mesquite beans or anything we found in and around the yard. We pretended for hours, limited only by our own imaginations.

Granddaddy understood the value of play. He loved checkers and won more than he lost. The grandchildren never presented even a slight challenge. He prohibited card or dice games because of the connection to gambling. Once his children introduced him to the game of Wahoo, the prohibition against dice lifted. He rarely lost at any game. When the competitive family gathered, they set up card tables and enjoyed spirited games of checkers, wahoo, dominos, or forty-two. Intense games allowed the entire family to escape the daily demands of work.

My mother focused most of her energy on work. Occasionally she escaped to music or sewing. Even her hobbies produced something of value. She rarely participated in anything just for fun. The sweet memory of her father and his special gift to her and her sister returned my mother to the carefree days of her childhood. She wistfully recalled the days when she played for the sheer joy of it.

Long before physicians discovered the importance of life-work balance to a healthy lifestyle, Granddaddy instinctively understood the value of rest and relaxation. However, he took games quite seriously. He *really* liked to win and *really* hated to lose.

Dooly

Origin – Gaelic, Irish
Meaning of the surname Dooly
12th century Gaelic meaning Dark Hero
Irish meaning hero with dark skin

Dupree

Origin – French
Meaning of the surname Dupree –
Topographical name of someone who
lived near a meadow

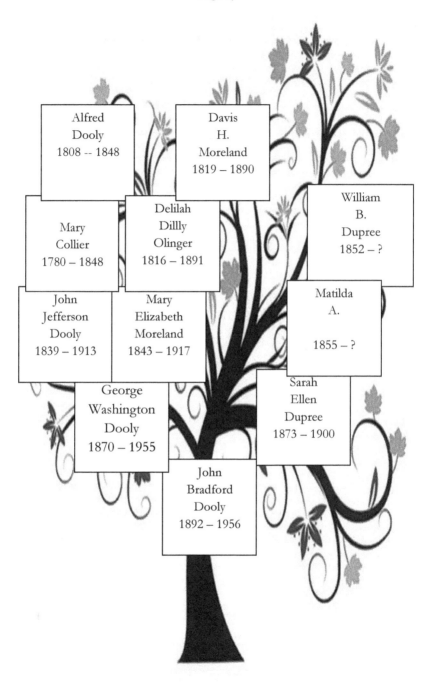

Alfred
Dooly
1808 -- 1848

Davis
H.
Moreland
1819 – 1890

William
B.
Dupree
1852 – ?

Mary
Collier
1780 – 1848

Delilah
Dillly
Olinger
1816 – 1891

Matilda
A.

1855 – ?

John
Jefferson
Dooly
1839 – 1913

Mary
Elizabeth
Moreland
1843 – 1917

George
Washington
Dooly
1870 – 1955

Sarah
Ellen
Dupree
1873 – 1900

John
Bradford
Dooly
1892 – 1956

The Life of a Sharecropper

John Bradford Dooly - PoPo (Pawpaw) Dooly

"Too often, parents whose children express an interest in farming squelch it because they envision dirt, dust, poverty, and hermit living. But great stories come out of great farming."
Joel Salatin

Before the Civil War, most people "worked the land" and owned the land they worked. This was especially true in Texas because of generous land grants from the Mexican government, the Republic of Texas, and from the United States after Texas joined the Union. Spanish officials enticed settlers with promises of land, religious tolerance, and special privileges. An immigrant in Mexican Texas received a *labor* (177 acres) of cropland and a *league* (4400 acres) of grazing land. In return for the land, the settler promised to obey the constitution of Mexico, practice Christianity, and prove good moral character. Those who came during the Texas Revolution received a *head right* of 640 acres just for arriving, plus 320 acres for each three-month's service in the army. Both governments of the Republic of Texas and the United States granted additional acres as payment of debts or reward for military service until the Civil War.

The promise of land ownership drove immigrants to leave the familiarity of their homes and families. In a 1913 essay, *How to Abolish Unfair Taxation*, Clarence Darrow wrote, "No man created the earth, but to a large extent all take from the earth a portion of it and mould it into useful things for the use of man. Without land man cannot live; without access to it man cannot labor."

Owning land gave the pioneers a place to call home – something worth defending. It established the family's place in society. Farmers formed an intensely personal connection to the land as they tilled the soil and cultivated the earth. They invested in the land while they established permanent settlements. The harvest afforded necessary provisions for the family and the community. Beyond the necessities of life, landownership offered position and status in local society. The dream of owning land with all the rights and responsibilities caused people to risk everything for the promise of a better life.

The Civil War changed everything. Many Texans never returned from the war. Some died, and others relocated to different states or nations. Some of the soldiers returned without funds to pay their taxes. Consequently, many property owners sold land to settle tax debts. By the 1870s, about seventy percent of farmers worked on land they did not own.

They became tenant farmers or sharecroppers, a term identifying chronically poor, often illiterate, farm families. The landowner provided land for farming; shelter for the sharecropper's family; necessities such as mules, plows, seeds; and most importantly, credit for living expenses until the harvest. The sharecropper provided his only resource – manual labor. When they settled up, the landowner received three-fourths of the yield and the sharecropper one-fourth.

From the landowner's perspective, this might seem fair, considering the lopsided investment of his resources.

However, the system perpetuated itself. The tenant families remained at the bottom of the socio-economic scale. The sharecropper required almost all his earnings to pay back debts for living expenses. Often, the sharecropper owed the landowner more than he could pay. He remained on the farm, each year hoping to realize enough profit to purchase his own land. Few sharecroppers ever broke the vicious cycle. Although, development of oil, railroading, and sawmilling industries provided some with alternatives, prospects remained scarce. Too often, they simply replaced bondage to the landowner to similar oppression by the company store.

World War II finally allowed sharecroppers an opportunity to break the cycle. Uncle Sam sent millions an invitation to a patriotic duty they could not refuse. Those unable to join the armed forces found work in shipyards and other defense industries. Few continued to work on the farms. After the war, the GI Bill provided previously unimagined educational opportunities and financial resources. Once out of the system, they chose to abandon farming – preferring to pursue a different American dream.

Dooly ancestors joined other Irish immigrants who sought a better life in America. Historical documents record spelling the surname Dooly a number of ways. Thomas O'Dooley, born 1670 in Ulster, Northwest, Ireland, immigrated at age 94 with his family to Augusta County, Virginia where he lived until his death on August 20, 1774 at age 104. Though records differ on the exact birth, immigration, and death dates, documentation clearly proves the American origin of the Dooly/Dooley bloodline began when Thomas O'Dooley and his son, Henry Dooley, his wife and eight children arrived in Virginia.

The Irish from 1700s Ulster experienced religious conflict, lack of political freedom, and dire economic conditions. America lured immigrants with promises of land ownership and greater religious freedom. Many financed passage to America by becoming indentured servants. Some skilled workers completed the period of servitude and assimilated into the life of the new nation. Others found life more difficult and struggled to achieve their dreams.

Although longevity appears to run in the family line, Henry died at the relatively young age of 62. Though his wife Martha, ten years his junior, outlived him by several years, she still died a young, 58 year old woman. The difficult voyage followed by a hard life in Colonial America took a toll on their health, and both died prematurely.

Throughout their lives, John and Gladys Dooly's sons spelled their surname differently. When one of the daughters inquired why, her father explained. "My teacher told me I was spelling my last name wrong. I got tired of arguing and of correcting people. So, I just gave up and let them spell it however they chose - Dooley."

Henry's sons, including the youngest, William Stephen Dooly, fought in the American Revolution. U.S. Revolutionary War Roles (1775-1783) list the Dooly siblings.

Prior to 1820, William moved his wife, Elizabeth Bush, and their nine children south from Virginia to rural Elbert County Georgia where he lived for the remainder of his life. Land titles record the sale of land to William's son, Mathew Dooly. Prior to the civil war, Mathew Dooly purchased land first in Tennessee and then in Talladega, Alabama. One of his fourteen children, Alfred, left home at the age of 22 and moved to Missouri. There he met and married a young woman named Dicey and fathered six children before he died as a forty-year-old young man.

Civil War records indicate that Alfred's son, John Jefferson Dooly, served as a private in the Union Army. Internment records in Fannin County, TX support his Civil War military service. In the decade following the war, he and his wife, Mary Moreland, relocated to Northeastern Texas, where they raised twelve children, and lived the remainder of their lives.

John Jefferson and Mary Elizabeth Dooly

Front Row Children: Maudie Allie, Etta May and Charles Henry Dooly (Children of William "Bill" Dooly and his wife Sarildia); Moses H. and John Franklin Spann (Children of Martha Ann "Mattie" and husband Moses Spann); Annie Thomas and William M "Will" Gann (Children of Eliza Jane and husband Isaac Gann). Back Row Adults: Sarildia Louisa "Lou" Dooly (nee Meray), wife of Bill, Bill Dooly, George Dooly, Daniel Dooly, John J. Dooly, Mary E. Dooly, Patsy Dooly, Martha Elizabeth Gann (daughter of Isaac Gann), Mattie Spann (nee Dooly), Moses Franklin Spann (husband of Mattie), Isaac Newton Gann (husband of Eliza Jane)

A ten-year-old child, George Washington Dooly moved with his parents, John and Mary, to Texas. He grew up in Northeast Texas and never strayed far from his boyhood home. Sarah Ellen Dupree's family moved to Northeast Texas when she was seven years old. Sarah and George likely knew each other as children, or perhaps they met as teenagers. The young sharecropper married an eighteen-year-old woman who bore three sons within five years. When Sarah died at age twenty-six, the young widower, George, struggled to raise his young sons, John, Samuel, and Daniel.

The eldest son, John Bradford, was only eight years old when his mother died and twelve when his father re-married and introduced the widow, Dorcas Elizabeth Duvalt Coomer Dooly, to his sons. She brought with her two sons, both younger than John. The next years brought two more children, a son, Roy, and a daughter, Esther Maye.

My grandmother recounted the story of a stepmother who cruelly mistreated John and his brothers. Historical family records paint a picture of a young widow with two sons, William and Jessie. In the fall of 1915, she buried two children, six year old, Esther Maye, her only daughter, and three weeks later, thirteen year old Jessie. The heartbroken mother struggled to understand the loss of her children. The other four children continued to look to her for care and guidance. Unable to cope with the overwhelming sense of grief, perhaps she unfairly blamed the boys for surviving while her babies died.

Eager to escape the abuse, the young John, scarcely more than a boy, left home. He pursued the only skill he knew – a skill he learned from his father. He worked the land. Since he had no means to purchase land, he became a sharecropper. He fell in love and married a twenty-one year old, Jewell Williams. The marriage lasted only four years, and Jewell bore no children. What happened? Family stories diverge. My grandmother spoke often of her sister, whom she reported died of "dropsy." This unscientific term leaves much to conjecture – perhaps a blood clot – perhaps congestive heart failure. Another relative described the cause of death as hemorrhage following a miscarriage. Because most people died at home and records rarely reported a medical cause of death, the mystery remained.

Four years later, John married my grandmother, the youngest sister of his first wife. Were the two girls anything alike? No one knows. Family stories provided no details of either courtship. Clues indicated differences in the girl's natural tendencies. Clearly, their physical appearance differed dramatically. The older statuesque sister stood erect and tall. In contrast, my petite grandmother, Gladys Virginia, measured less than five feet tall.

At a time in history when most young women married in their teens, Gladys remained single at age twenty-six. She and her family feared she might never marry. She resigned herself to the role of caregiver for her widowed mother. The couple's marriage provided the answer to the young woman's prayers. He cared for her and for her mother.

The year following their marriage, the couple welcomed a son, Garland. Gladys' siblings encouraged John with stories of plentiful job opportunities and affordable land. John found work on the Boaz family farm near Noodle. Like many other sharecroppers, he hoped to save enough money to purchase his own farm. Within a year of their move to West Texas, they welcomed another son. Out of respect and honor to his father, John and Gladys named their second son for his grandfather, George. Gladys adored her husband, sons, and mother and devotedly cared for her family.

John defied the stereotypical hotheaded, quick tempered, hard drinking Irish Catholic. Only his thick curly auburn hair evidenced his Irish heritage. From all accounts, his strong moral compass set an example for his sons. The strong, quiet man of character embraced the Baptist faith and never drank alcohol. Hard working and patient, he rarely lost his temper. Family and friends respected him as an honest man of integrity.

The tenant farmhouse seemed quite large to a little girl. It consisted of a kitchen, the essential hub of the home where everyone gathered to eat, talk, and share the events of life. The other two rooms served as a place to sleep. A wrap-around, screened-in porch surrounded the house. West Texas farm homes of the 1940s and 1950s lacked air conditioners. Only wealthy families could afford fans. The porch took advantage of the evening breeze and provided the most comfortable place to sit and visit. When the adult children visited, they set up cots and slept on the porch.

My grandparents slept in an ornately carved, pale yellow, double bed. A matching dressing table and contrasting chifforobe completed the furnishings in the sparsely decorated bedroom. I loved sleeping in what felt like an enormous bed between my MoMo and PoPo Dooly. Bedtime represented a fun time with PoPo. He loved to hear his granddaughter laugh. We shared a special game.

The big man sat upright in the bed, bonked his head on the headboard. "Ouch!" he moaned with all the flair of a Hollywood actor, while I squealed with delight.

He continued to howl in pain while I giggled uncontrollably. He never seemed to tire of this game, which continued until some other adult turned out the lights and forced us to go to sleep.

My PoPo loved to make his granddaughters laugh. Simple games delighted me. One particularly favorite game involved hide and seek with PoPo pretending not to be able to catch me as I dashed through the house. My forehead still bears a scar as evidence of that game gone wrong. A game of chase ended abruptly when my head collided with the corner of the dressing table. Wet cloths absorbed the gushing blood and held pressure until the oozing stopped. I remember no pain, only the abrupt end to a fun game of chase. PoPo deferred the responsibility for my injury to an inanimate object. I vividly remember the event as PoPo slammed his hand against the table and scolded it for hurting his baby girl.

Each time we visited, he delighted in jiggling change in his pockets. He hid the coins in the deep pockets of his overalls. He teased his granddaughters with the promise of a shiny coin. We dug deep into the side pockets, searching until we found the reward. As a four year old, I had no concept of money, or the sacrifice even a quarter represented.

**The Dooly family:
Gladys, George, John, Garland**

Death cut short memories of my PoPo. He spent his entire adult life as a sharecropper or tenant farmer and never owned the land he farmed. He died in his sixties when I was only four years old. Discrepancies surface between the storied history and the actual historical medical records. Though my grandmother described a gastrointestinal hemorrhage as the result of a bleeding ulcer, the death certificate records a pulmonary embolus following surgery for an enlarged prostate. No one expected the routine procedure to result in my grandfather's demise.

Life changed dramatically for his devastated widow, whose world centered on him. He provided and cared for her. She faced life without the love of her life and without skills or money.

As I consider the legacy passed down from my paternal grandfather many intangibles come to mind. He taught by example the value of an honest day's work. He modeled a sense of joy in the simple things of life.

I understood my value through his eyes. He enthusiastically welcomed me into his presence. He lavished time and attention on me. Better than any monetary inheritance, PoPo left me the memory of a benevolent grandfather who loved to make his granddaughter happy and delighted in hearing my laughter. He treated me like the princess he believed me to be.

The Legend of Tom Dooley

"Hang down your head Tom Dooley
Hang down your head and cry
Hang down your head Tom Dooley
Poor boy you're bound to die."
Old North Carolina Folksong by Thomas C. Land
Recorded by multiple artists including the 1958 version by
the Kingston Trio

"Is Tom your uncle?"

The scene repeated itself each time I introduced myself. Though I anticipated the taunt, my body responded involuntarily. A sensation of heat began in my neck and rose steadily to my reddening face. I hated the song and its negative image. My brother on the other hand, loved every bit of the attention and determined Tom would be the name of one of his future sons.

In 1958, the Kingston Trio, a popular folk group, recorded the song romanticizing the tragic life of a poor Appalachian boy. Inspired by the popularity of the song, Michael Landon portrayed Tom Dooley in the fictionalized movie version. The song and movie kept the legend alive well into the 1960's. I heard the chorus of the song almost every day during junior high and high school.

Imagine my relief to disprove any ancestral link to Tom Dooley. Folk legends seldom concern themselves with facts. This legend sacrificed facts for the sake of a good story. With retelling over the years, the sordid tale grew more scandalous.

The real Tom, a former Confederate soldier, Thomas C. Dula, (June 22, 1845 – May 1, 1868) engaged in multiple sexual relationships, which proved his ruin. The tragic story, fueled by national newspaper coverage of Tom's trial for the murder of Laura Foster in North Carolina, proved an enduring legend.

The true story, a murder mystery, resulted from shockingly complicated sexual exploits. Born in abject poverty to an Appalachian hill country family in North Carolina, Tom grew up the youngest of three brothers and one younger sister, Eliza. He attended school and likely played with the neighbor's children, a family of cousins, Anne, Laura, and Pauline Foster.

Tom and Anne became intimate. Anne's mother discovered the two in bed together, when they were barely in their teens. Tom earned quite a reputation as a ladies' man.

Three months before his 18th birthday, Tom joined the Confederate army and served as a private in Company K in the 42nd North Carolina Infantry Regiment. Tom's Civil War muster card lists him as a musician and a drummer. Perhaps he utilized his musical talents on the fiddle and banjo to attract female admirers.

Before the war, Anne Foster, a local beauty and Tom's first love, married an older neighbor, James Melton. Mr. Melton also joined the Confederate army and distinguished himself by fighting in the Battle of Gettysburg. Union forces captured both Melton and Dula. After the war, the union released both soldiers, and they returned home. Mr. Melton, a successful cobbler and farmer, no longer desired a physical relationship with his much younger wife. He invited Tom to join him and Anne in their cabin. With the older gentleman's consent, Tom and Anne began sharing a bed in the home, while James slept alone.

When Anne's cousin, Pauline Foster, returned to the area, she moved into the Melton household as a hired servant. Tom lived up to his reputation and soon initiated an affair with Pauline. Anne didn't seem to mind and reportedly, the three shared a bed in the small cabin. Mr. Melton still slept alone.

As if this wasn't complicated enough, Tom Dula soon reconnected with another Foster cousin. Laura tempted Tom's sexual appetite, and enticed him into yet another new affair completely separate from his arrangements in Melton cabin. Splitting his time between Laura and the women in the Melton household seemed to keep Dula happy and probably exhausted.

Did these people have no moral compass? Surely, the fine women of the community shunned the Foster women and excluded them from social events. Whispers and disapproving stares followed them as they entered the general store. "Did you hear? They are all sharing a bed with the same man. Poor James – it's a shame he's so blind to what's going on right under his nose."

What was wrong with these people! Even by modern standards, they lacked even a hint of common decency.

Unknown to Tom, a more sinister reason prompted Pauline's decision to return home. Escapades during her travels resulted in a serious infection. She returned home and urgently sought treatment for syphilis. She failed to inform her new partner, and soon Tom exhibited symptoms. Because his symptoms occurred shortly after he began visiting Laura, Tom erroneously blamed her and vowed revenge. According to folklore, Laura became pregnant and planned to elope with Tom. Perhaps he agreed to Laura's plan in order to lure the young woman away and exact his revenge.

Laura disappeared on May 25, 1866. That morning, her father woke to discover both his daughter and his prized horse, Belle, missing. The horse returned the next day, but Laura did not. After several weeks, searchers discovered the rope used to tie Foster's horse to a tree on bloodstained ground not far from Tom Dula's home. Suspicion immediately fell on Dula, who fled for Tennessee and assumed a new name, Tom Hall.

Perhaps not so coincidentally, Pauline also visited Tennessee. When she returned home, a friend jokingly inquired if she had left because she had killed Laura. Pauline laughed nervously and quipped, "We killed her together."

Law enforcement officers, not taking the confession lightly, arrested Pauline, and charged her as an accessory to murder. Fearing for her life, the woman told lawmen everything she knew. She testified, "Dula and Anne killed Laura together."

She led them to a shallow grave in the woods, and authorities found a badly decomposed corpse, only identifiable by Laura's clothing. Evidence revealed a vicious stab wound under the left breast into the heart.

Pauline supplied specific details of the murder. Despite the fact that Pauline led them to the grave and gave witness to first hand information, the sheriff released her. Prosecutors never charged her with a crime. If she participated in her sister's murder, she eluded consequences.

A search party doggedly pursued Tom to Tennessee. They found him working on the farm of Colonel James Grayson. The posse enlisted Grayson's assistance. The Colonel persuaded Tom to surrender and return to Wilkes County to stand trial.

In a surprising move, which brought the case to national attention, former North Carolina Governor Zebulon Vance volunteered to represent Dula *pro bono*. News stories painted the Yadkin Valley as a decadent lair of free love and promiscuity. The complicated details of Dula's sex life created a public frenzy for the salacious details. The trial became a national sensation.

The prosecutor presented a strong case. A physician testified to treating Tom, Anne, and Pauline for syphilis. Tom's own words proved the most damaging. Multiple witnesses swore to hearing Tom vow vengeance. Several men heard him say, "I'll do in the woman who gave me the pock."

Ironically, Pauline, not Laura, infected Tom, who then spread the disease to Anne and Laura.

The evidence convinced the jury. They convicted Tom of murder and sentenced him to death. A separate jury acquitted Anne Melton.

Historical reports failed to document a clear cause of Mrs. Melton's death. She suffered a carriage accident shortly before her death. However, complications of syphilis plagued her throughout her life. Although she escaped execution and maintained her innocence until her death in 1874, rumors followed her to the grave. Many believed she, not Dula, dealt the final blow ending Laura Foster's life.

Reports of the condemned man's last words vary. The young man reportedly wrote a fifteen-page account of his life and a note exonerating Anne of Laura's murder. This version romanticizes his commitment to his first love. His ability to read or write seems unlikely given the poverty of his upbringing and his station in life.

In another account, he upheld his innocence. As he stood on the gallows facing death, Dula declared, "Gentlemen, do you see this hand? I didn't harm a hair on the girl's head."

At Dula's hanging on May 1, 1868 in Statesville, other witnesses reported his last words, "You have such a nice clean rope, I ought to have washed my neck."

Shortly after the execution, a local poet named Thomas C Land wrote the folksong, *Tom Dooley,* the Appalachian pronunciation of Dula. The literary account of the tragedy combined with the widespread publicity of the trial further cemented a place in North Carolina legend.

Interestingly enough, though the more romantic version of the story propelled them to fame, the members of the Kingston Trio knew the sordid story of Tom Dooley, and delighted in sharing the details with various house crews they met on tour.

In 2001, an unofficial action without legal force acquitted Tom Dula of all charges after a petition circulated around Wilkes County and the county seat.

The tragic story continued to provide material for music and literature. In 2011, Sharyn McCrumb wrote a novel, *The Ballad of Tom Dooley*. With available evidence, she reconstructed a fictionalized account of events surrounding the murder of Laura Foster. Over the years, popular music continued to reference the tragic figure and kept the legend alive.

The branches of the Dooly family tree may contain some unsavory characters. Skeletons lurk in every family's hidden corners. However, this particular skeleton hangs on a different family tree. No evidence connects our Dooly family with the legendary Tom Dula, AKA Tom Dooley.

Williams

English, Scottish, Irish, Welsh
Meaning of the surname Williams –
Soldier in the king's army
Alternate meaning – of strong mind

Morgan

Gaelic, Celtic predates Christianity,
dating to the middle ages
Meaning of the surname Morgan –
Lives by the sea

Adoniram D. Williams 1828 – 1888

Barzilla Graves Morgan 1829 – 1894

Jincy May Holloway 1837 – 1901

Mary Carolyn Spradlin 1828 – 1901

James Henry Williams 1864 – 1911

Nancy Elizabeth Morgan 1862 – 1957

Gladys Virginia Williams 1898 –1987 1987

The Art of Care Giving

Gladys Virginia Williams Dooly

"It is not how much you do;
It is how much love you put in the doing."
Mother Teresa

Pictures of a young Gladys reveal a beautiful young woman with an oval face and sharp chiseled features. Full breasts seemed out of place on her tiny frame. She stood 4'10" and never weighed more than 120 pounds. Years of hard work, disappointment and pain exacted a toll. If finances allowed her to purchase store bought clothes, her frugal nature held her back. She made

Gladys Virginia Williams Dooly

her own clothing to save money for other necessities. Her wardrobe consisted of several serviceable shirtwaist dresses. A heavily starched and ironed apron completed the daily attire.

Still single at the age of twenty-six, perhaps Gladys wondered if her dream of a husband and children could still come true. The prospects seemed slim. Could she dare dream of a future with her sister's widower, John Dooly?

She knew him well. A kind man, he lovingly cared for her sister, Jewel, until her death. Could she expect him to love and care for her the same way?

The tall statuesque Jewell looked nothing like her petite younger sister. Gladys' subservient personality contrasted with Jewell's independent spirit. She recalled her sister's dying words. Jewell wanted her baby sister to marry John and give him children. "He's a good man. He will learn to love you. He'll take care of you and of Mother. He will be lonely. Promise me – you'll take care of him."

The girls' mother, Bettie, encouraged the courtship, confident that John would care and provide for her youngest daughter.

Life handed the family matriarch, Bettie, a series of losses. Her husband, James, died as a young man, leaving Bettie to raise a large family. Their marriage produced ten children. Besides Jewell, she buried other daughters. Twin girls, Eula and Bula, died in infancy. Eventually, she followed her adult children to Noodle, Texas, where she lived the remainder of her life with her youngest daughter.

Gladys happily dedicated the early years of her married life to making a home for her husband, sons, and aging mother. She lived by the motto; *idle hands are the devil's workshop*. She determined to leave the devil no room to work in her life. No stranger to hard work, Gladys willingly labored in the fields beside her husband and sons. Certainly, she expected to live out her days caring for her husband and working beside him on the farm. However, fate dealt cruel blows, and she found herself without a husband, without means, and responsible for the care of her elderly, demented mother.

When John died, Gladys not only lost her husband and life partner, she also lost the home they shared. The terms of living as tenants on the farm required the sharecropper's family to produce a crop. Her sons struggled to raise their own families. The absence of the primary breadwinner, the farmer who worked the land, meant his widow's relocation. Facing eviction, Gladys remained focused on her concern for her elderly mother. She often referred to the alternative as an "Old Folk's Home" a place she adamantly declared she'd never allow her mother to live. She found a small cottage for rent and moved with her mother to Abilene.

Momo scurried about the house dividing attention between grandchildren and her elderly mother. She rarely sat down. Flitting from place to place and task to task, she constantly talked to anyone who would listen, and often to no one in particular. When no one else listened, she conversed with herself, the television, or some unseen guest. She tirelessly went about her tasks and rarely sat down in a chair. Occasionally she sat long enough to watch her favorite soap opera, *Days of Our Lives*. The cast of characters became as real to her as her own family.

Dementia robbed both women – Nancy Elizabeth depended on her youngest daughter, to meet her every need. The younger woman selflessly provided care without complaining. She lovingly bathed, fed, and met the daily needs of her ninety-year-old mother. She met the challenge without formal training, outside resources or recognition.

Gladys lived with constant fear and anxiety. Fear of intruders – fear of not having enough – fear of storms – fear her mother might get out of the house and wander away. She feared Bettie would lose her balance, fall and experience a hip fracture, a problem she solved by securing her mother to the rocking chair with soft rag straps.

Gladys, the caregiver, never took a day off. She never traveled. She slept lightly so she heard every change in breathing and every movement. When Bettie could no longer attend church, Gladys stayed home with her. Television preachers became her ministers. She tirelessly worked to assure a safe environment for the mother whom she idolized. She recounted stories of their shared past, oblivious to the fact that Bettie no longer understood the words she said. The one person who shared her memories could no longer speak meaningfully about their experiences.

After Grandmother Williams died, Momo moved in with our family. She assumed the role of caregiver for her grandchildren. She continued the same hurried pace, never still or quite for a moment. Four rambunctious children tested her tenuous grip on sanity. Sibling rivalry pushed her to the edge of reason. "You children are raising my blood pressure," she would repeat almost daily while splashing water on top of her head to bring her blood pressure down. "You're going to make me have a stroke."

Unfortunately, her threats failed to stop the fights, which frequently became physical. Momo's belief in the superiority of males did little to ease the conflicts between my brother and me. Her steadfast conviction of women's subservient role clashed with the raising of three strong-willed granddaughters.

Eventually, the children outgrew their need for a caregiver and Momo moved to her own little apartment. She established a sense of independence. Despite the years of our terrorizing her, she loved us anyway.

In the process of a move, Mother cleaned out our toy box. The baby doll meant nothing to her. I outgrew playing with dolls and had no emotional attachment. Momo found it and retrieved it from the trash heap. She recalled a day she sent the doll home with me.

"Please take the baby doll home, and don't bring it back to my house." Momo begged. "It upsets Grandmother. She cradles the baby doll and rocks it. In her mind, it's a real baby. She worries and cries because the baby is abandoned and has no one to care for it. I can't stand to see her tortured over the doll."

She took the baby to her apartment and kept it as a tangible reminder of the days she spent caring for her own mother. I suspect she shed tears remembering how Grandmother rocked the baby and cried. She repaired rips and lovingly dressed the baby in clothes she found at a second-hand store. "This was your mother's baby doll. I want you to have it," she told my daughter as she presented it to her great-granddaughter as one of her prized treasures.

Today the doll wears a dress once worn by my daughter and occupies a special place in our home.

Momo labored as a caregiver before anyone bestowed a title to the position. She attended to the needs of her family without complaining. Did she have caregiver stress? Most definitely. Did she receive appreciation or recognition? Not in this world. Was she perfect? Hardly. However, she assumed the caregiver role without question. She instinctively cared for the needs of her family and in doing so; found fulfillment – the purpose for her life and a labor of love.

A Well-Kept Secret

Based on stories shared at the Williams Family Reunion by
descendants of
Nancy Elizabeth Morgan Reeves Williams

Nancy Elizabeth Morgan Williams with her youngest son, Ray

"Three may keep a secret, if two of them are dead."
Benjamin Franklin, Poor Richard's Almanac

The young bride released a sigh of relief as her husband strode toward the blacksmith shop. Hot tears spilled from her sad blue eyes. He would be gone at least eight hours. She reassured herself. *As long as he's at work, I'm safe.*

Her marriage looked so different from the example her parents lived. She sobbed harder as she thought about her father. *I'm glad he isn't alive to witness the mess I've made of my life.*

Despite the eight-year age difference, she expected to build a good life with the handsome young man. Like her parents, he came from Kentucky. Her mother wholeheartedly approved of her marriage. Perhaps her family wondered if she would ever find a husband. At the age of twenty-two, her prospects lessened. Hardworking and financially secure, Elijah Reeves represented everything she wanted in a husband. He courted her, respected her mother, and fit in with her brothers. Prior to the marriage, he hid his dark side from her and from her family.

Within days of the wedding, everything changed. The charming public person differed drastically from the cruel man who shared her home and her bed. When he walked through the door, his surly side surfaced. He criticized her abilities as a homemaker. Slamming his fist on the dinner table, he snarled. "You know I hate turnip greens. Your mother is an excellent cook. Didn't you learn anything?"

She heard him greet the neighbors cheerfully. *How can his mood change so quickly? How could I have been so wrong?*

Each day she worked diligently. Everything needed to be exactly to his liking – the house in order and dinner ready with his favorite foods. Every evening she prayed for peace. Nothing she did pleased him, and she failed to understand why. Trapped and terrified of this man, she lived in constant fear. Each day his anger escalated. His temper worsened and the outbursts became increasingly physical. He threw things, often in her direction.

When the coffee cup hurled in her direction crashed to the floor, he stomped to her cowering form and grabbed her hair. Seething with anger, his eyes filled with disgust and hatred. He lifted her to her feet and effortlessly threw her across the room. He formed a fist but stopped short of striking her face. He refused to leave visible evidence of his cruelty. He stormed through the front door still shaking with rage from the encounter.

Because she hid her misery so well, Bettie wondered if anyone would believe her. The neighbors respected him as a hard working provider. Publically, he treated her like a princess and carefully limited the physical damage so no one suspected the abuse. Even her family had no idea what happened in the privacy of their little cabin. The stigma and cost of divorce ensnared her, like many nineteenth century women, in an abusive marriage. She hated to admit defeat, but fear outweighed her pride.

Recently, Elijah slept with an ax and a gun under the bed. When she asked for an explanation, his silence frightened her even more. His size intimidated her. Thoughts flooded her mind as she considered her limited options. *I know this is going to get worse. Maybe he'll kill me, and then I'll be free. I can't defend myself. He's twice my size. How can I possibly escape? Mother will be here in the morning. She'll know something is wrong. I can't pretend any longer. I'll tell Mother everything. She'll help me figure out what to do.*

Mrs. Morgan planned her weekly visit to town for supplies to include time for a visit to her only daughter's little cabin. The mother and daughter shared a close bond and often communicated without words. Mary arrived as expected and immediately felt the tension. The women's eyes connected, and hot tears spilled from Bettie's eyes. The mother secured the door, enfolded her daughter in her arms, and waited for a break in the torrent of tears. "What's wrong? Tell me about it," she urged.

The young bride poured out her heart. She fully trusted her mother to listen and understand. A new round of uncontrollable sobs racked her body. She trembled with fear as she recalled the most recent abuse. She provided details of the attack. "I try so hard. Nothing I do is right. He hates me. I don't know what to do. I'm afraid – afraid he is going to kill me!"

They wept freely. Eventually sadness and guilt gave way to rage. Words tumbled out unfiltered. "I should have never encouraged you to marry him. I am so sorry, sweet baby girl. He can't get away with this. I'd like to kill him myself. I'm afraid your brother's will beat him to death. Then they'd go to jail or worse. He isn't worth it." Fury fueled an action plan. "You can't spend one more night in this house. You deserve better, and he will not hurt you again! I promise. Pack your things, I will send your brothers to get you this evening."

Bettie spent the rest of the day following her mother's instructions. She hurriedly packed her clothes and a few personal items. *I must be done before Elijah gets home from work. I wonder how he will react. He is so unpredictable.* She imagined possibilities and shuddered at the thought of an encounter. Though her husband cared little for her, he valued his public image. Surely, he wouldn't risk a showdown with her brothers, who outnumbered him four to one.

The band of brothers arrived early that evening. With guns visible, they collected their sister and her belongings. Elijah stood at the door and without protest watched them leave.

At the edge of the road, Bettie turned for one last look at her husband and the home they shared. Their eyes met and one final smirk on Elijah's face assured the young woman. *I've made the right decision,* she thought as she walked toward an uncertain future.

Shortly after the encounter with the Morgan brothers, the handsome young man left Hunt County. Searches of marriage and divorce records failed to produce documentation of the legal end of the Reeves marriage. By November 1895, with or without benefit of an official divorce, he married Annie. They lived the rest of their lives in the panhandle of Texas. (Pampa, TX)

The young couple's relationship remains a mystery. Did he really consider murdering his bride? Were the gun and ax for a legitimate purpose? Did he regret marrying Bettie and find love with Annie? Did Bettie imagine the threats? Did she marry him to avoid spinster status? Were her fears warranted?

Bettie resolved to remain a single woman caring for her widowed mother. However, life changed when she met and married James Williams four years later. During their twenty-three year marriage, Bettie delivered ten children, seven surviving to adulthood. Before she reached her 50th birthday, James died, leaving her a young widow.

She served as the honored and much loved matriarch of her family. She lived a very long life, dying at the age of ninety-six. Her children lovingly cared for her. The stories of Bettie's early life remained a mystery. If her children knew the secret, they guarded it well.

Ninetieth Birthday Celebration for Betty Williams

Stitched With Grace

"Anyone who works on a quilt, who devotes her time, energy, creativity, and passion to that art, learns to value the work of her hands. And as any quilter will tell you, a quilter's quilting friends are some of the dearest, most generous, and most supportive people she knows."
Jennifer Chiaverini

I spoke with my stepmother, Linda, regularly in the days following the funeral. During his long battle with lung cancer, Daddy prepared for the move to his heavenly home and understood how to let go of the stuff he no longer needed. Over the last few months, he designated specific items for each of his children. At the end of the phone call she asked, "When can you come to the house? I want to give you the things your dad set aside for you and your sisters?"

With a heavy heart, I dutifully drove three-hours and parked my car in the long driveway. I swallowed hard as the knot in my throat tightened. A sob of regret and grief threatened to escape. *Why didn't I spend more time with Daddy when I had the chance?*

We carefully sorted through books, pictures, ties, and memorabilia. At the end of the day, she directed me to the guest room closet where I found three well-worn, fragile quilts. "Your grandmother made these quilts. Your Daddy wanted each of you girls to have one of them."

As we said our goodbyes, I placed the quilts in the trunk of my Toyota Corolla. "I'll let Patty and Lisa pick. I'm happy with any of the three."

When I returned home, I rearranged the quilts on the rack to make room for the latest addition. I lovingly examined the other four in my collection and visualized the hands of each woman who created these warm covers. Momo Dooly - Granny Carr - Granmommie Cargile – my mother-in-love, Melba Strange, women whose example of enduring difficult circumstances inspired me.

Our grandmothers sewed quilts during the Great Depression. Historians referred to the era as the quilt revival. Newspaper columns, magazine articles, pattern books, and catalogs disseminated quilt patterns to rural and city homes. Many quilts created during this period display the same pattern. Two of the most popular included Double Wedding Ring and Sunbonnet Sue. The Depression Era Block pattern often utilized recycled materials. The rural farm wife wasted nothing – embracing the motto – *Waste not, want not.* They utilized every available resource, making do with what they gathered – recycled clothing, small fabric scraps, and feed sacks.

We inherited little from the Williams/Dooly side of our family. Each of us received one of Momo's meager possessions. Patty treasured the trunk where our grandmother kept her do-dads. She placed treasures in discarded boxes and secured them with rubber bands. One special box held a collection of buttons that entertained her granddaughters for hours.

The chifforobe served as a closet for Momo's dresses. She never wore pants. A humble woman, she checked her image only to make sure her slip didn't hang below her shirtwaist dress. Lisa claimed the fragile piece as her treasured memento...

The Montgomery Ward treadle sewing machine enabled Momo to construct quilts to protect her family against the bitter winter temperatures. As I hung the quilt, I remembered Momo Dooly, a diminutive woman, seated at the machine, now located in the corner of my bedroom. Her legs pumped frantically and made the needle fly. One by one, she added the small squares of cloth and concerned herself less with artistry than purpose. The finished product provided warmth against the cold West Texas winds.

While the result supplied an essential need, quilt making also provided diversion from the hard times of the Great Depression. A woman escaped her daily troubles while concentrating on her stitches. Quilting fulfilled a need to be thrifty, industrious, and artistic. During difficult times, quilting parties offered the chance to socialize, gossip, and accomplish a shared goal. A group of ladies might complete several quilts in a day, instead of working individually on the project for weeks or months. Often women gathered to create a new quilt as a wedding gift for a new bride. The quilting bee served as a primary social contact for women and provided an integral element in the social fabric of rural communities.

Each of my inherited quilts represents the depression era. Granmommie's artistry in the Wedding Ring pattern mesmerizes me. Granny constructed an Around the World

Depression Era Block quilt from small uniform scraps of cloth. Momo joined odds and ends of material in no particular pattern to produce serviceable covers. Melba created the Sunbonnet Sue quilt after her retirement in the early 1980s. For her, the pattern symbolized her childhood years in the depression. With each stitch, she remembered her mother, aunts, sisters, and women who taught her the art of quilting.

"I had so much fun, choosing the fabrics and making the dresses," Melba beamed as she unfolded the quilt top. "It felt like playing paper dolls."

Unlike her mother, Melba didn't have to "make do" with the ragbag and scraps. She had the luxury of selecting the fabrics, matching solids with patterns, and dressing each Sunbonnet Sue luxuriously. As I caress the quilt, I feel my sweet mother-in-love's spirit. I reflect on her life. She grew up in the depression, raised by a widowed single mother – supported her husband and brothers as they served in World War II – raised two children – worked hard – loved her family. She embraced me with love and unconditional support as I grew from an adolescent bride to a confident wife and mother. The colorful artistic creation provides a tangible reminder of the encouragement she offered.

Instead of serving the purpose for which our families created them, the precious heirlooms now hang on a quilt rack and decorate a corner of my bedroom. How many hands shared in the making of each masterpiece? How many fingers bled after an errant needle stick? How many children snuggled beneath the warmth of these covers? Before retiring for the night, the family extinguished all open fires in the house. The wear and tear of the tattered, faded quilts evidences the fulfillment of their intended purpose.

Though I failed to inherit my predecessor's passion for sewing – for creating art pieces from fabric, I value the artistry represented. Each quilted treasure holds sweet memories of the special ladies who incorporated grace and love in every stitch.

Blessed are the children of the piecemakers...
For they shall inherit the quilts!
Unknown

Stories of the Next Generation

"There is a mysterious cycle in human events. To some generations much is given. Of other generations, much is expected. This generation of Americans has a rendezvous with destiny."
Franklin D. Roosevelt

Rebel in White

Clara Faye Deutschman Nadin Garrett

"I solemnly pledge myself before God and in the presence of this assembly, to pass my life in purity and to practice my profession faithfully. I will abstain from whatever is deleterious and mischievous, and will not take or knowingly administer any harmful drug. I will do all in my power to maintain and elevate the standard of my profession, and will hold in confidence all personal matters committed to my keeping and all family affairs coming to my knowledge in the practice of my calling. With loyalty will I endeavor to aid the physician in his work, and devote myself to the welfare of those committed to my care."
Florence Nightingale Pledge 1893

Two treasured textbooks, *Obstetrics* and *Anatomy and Physiology,* decorate the bookshelf in my home library. These books, given to me by my aunt as I entered nursing school over three decades ago, serve as a physical reminder of the sacrifice and dedication required to fulfill the dream of becoming a nurse – the dream and career Aunt Clara and I shared.

Did some event in the family cause her to drop out of high school? What compelled her to leave home? How long did she flounder before finding the calling that would become her life's work? Had she already tried and failed to make it on her own? When did she decide on the career path and what fueled her desire to pursue a career in nursing? Why did John Carr vehemently oppose his eldest stepdaughter's career decision?

Speculation fuels my imagination with reasons why the young woman dropped out of high school and left home. Though she loved her parents dearly, the independent, strong-willed woman yearned for freedom from the discipline of a strict stepfather. Maybe she tired of the responsibilities as the eldest daughter, caring for her younger siblings. Possibly, she followed a handsome young suitor, only to face disappointment as the romance soured before it developed. Perhaps she simply grew weary of the repetitive work of the family farm and longed for an urban existence. Even the nearby towns of Sweetwater and Abilene seemed large compared to the small West Texas community. Whatever her reasons, the resilient young woman faced family disapproval, defied her parents, and left the farm.

Letters from her brothers serving in the military filled her head with stories of travel to exotic places she longed to experience. Had she already decided on a career path requiring defiance of her family and risking her stepfather's disapproval? Each conjecture reveals another dimension of Aunt Clara's adolescent personality.

Her mother stood stoically in the yard. She gazed at the empty dirt road long after the car disappeared over the hill. Taking a handkerchief from her apron pocket, Verna brushed away an unbidden tear and wiped her nose. She nervously twisted the small square of cloth. Her first born was no longer under her watchful eye, but then the free-spirited young woman never acquiesced to the norms of the rural community.

She felt a twinge of guilt at her sense of relief. Tonight she would not be torn between loyalty to her husband and love for her daughter. Recent arguments turned the usually peaceful home to vocal battleground. Verna certainly understood her husband's concerns. John adamantly opposed Clara's decision to pursue a nursing career. Both Verna and John envisioned traditional roles for their daughters. They expected the girls to marry young men of reputable character and establish families of their own. Trying to dissuade Clara, her stepfather shared his experiences of caring for the sick, emphasizing the demands nursing required. The thought of their daughter caring for the private needs of men challenged the family's conservative principles.

Despite her misgivings, Verna harbored a secret pride in Clara's determination to pursue her dream. Hadn't she raised her to be independent, and encouraged the characteristics of determination and tenacity? Her daughter possessed everything she needed to succeed. The mother prayed for strength to let go. She turned around, opened the door to the farmhouse, and refocused her energies on the daily demands of running the family farm and raising the five younger children. No time to dwell on her emotions, she returned to the kitchen and prepared lunch.

Even in the 1940's admission to nursing school required a high school diploma. Clara's first order of business – earn a high school diploma – not as simple as it might sound. She had to earn the money to live in a boarding house in Abilene. Too old to attend high school, she solved the dilemma by presenting herself to be younger than her actual age. Abilene High School's yearbook, *The Flashlight,* reveals a picture of the twenty-three year old graduate. She obviously fit in, appearing no older than the other students. She involved herself in student life by singing in the Glee Club. Other activities evidenced her passion for nursing. She supported the American war effort by volunteering with a student group, *War Work, Bonds and Stamps* and *Surgical Bandages.* As a graduating senior in the AHS class of 1943, Clara indicated her intention to attend West Texas Nurse Training.

In 1943, World War II created a critical nursing shortage in the United States. The government established the Cadet Nurse Corps. Student nurses received training and a stipend in exchange for a promise to be available for service if needed. Serving in the Army Nurse Corps allowed Clara and other young women like her to gain valuable training while serving their country. The students' orientation to military nursing taught them to prepare for gas injuries. They learned to create a bivouac (a temporary camp without tents or cover.) Their instruction included how to seek foxholes for cover and methods for purifying water. The student's salary of $15 a month increased with the individuals rank to a maximum of $60 a month. The service of thousands of cadets remains on record as an exceptional contribution to the United States during and following World War II.

Two years of service in the Army Nurse Corps filled the years from Clara's high school graduation and enrollment in the three-year diploma-nursing program in Fort Worth, Texas. Her nursing textbooks document the dates of nursing school attendance. On the inside cover, Clara Faye Deutschman wrote her name, St. Joseph Nursing School, 1947. St. Joseph Hospital and Nursing School founded in 1906, stood as a landmark in Fort Worth, Texas for many years. Aunt Clara proudly wore the cap and pin of St. Joseph. The state board of nursing records the date of her registered nursing license as 1948.

Nursing students of the 1940-50s entering three year training programs paid no tuition, but were required to purchase nursing textbooks at a cost of approximately $55. Nursing students lived in the on-site nurse's residence throughout their three years of training. The school reported results of all course examinations to the students' parents, who signed and returned the forms to the nursing school. The school maintained a monthly weight record of all students.

Upon entrance to the program, the nursing student provided her own incidentals, which included:

- one pair of bandage scissors
- one pair of white nurses shoes ($8.00)
- two pairs of white nylons (at $1.00 each)
- three nurse dresses (approximately $4.75 each)
- six collars (at 35¢ each)
- fourteen aprons (at $2.50 each)
- one alarm clock
- one wrist watch
- one napkin ring
- one steamer rug or colored blanket
- two labeled cotton laundry bags (20 inches by 20 inches)
- Nurses were also required to purchase a cape after six months, which in the 1950s cost anywhere from $21-$30.

After graduating, salaries for mid-century nurses averaged $140 per month, but some hospitals paid as little as $90 per month. Many hospitals employed only single women, a practice continued well into the 1960s in some communities. Up until then, many married graduates worked as private-duty nurses. The average workweek for nurses at this time was 48 hours but ranged from 66 to 90 hours.

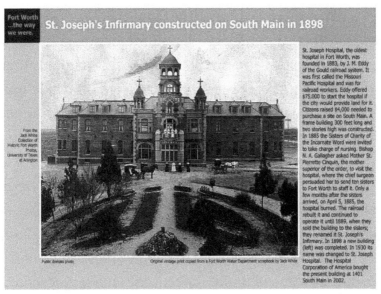

Fort Worth ...the way we were. **St. Joseph's Infirmary constructed on South Main in 1898**

St. Joseph Hospital, the oldest hospital in Fort Worth, was founded in 1883, by J. M. Eddy of the Gould railroad system. It was first called the Missouri Pacific Hospital and was for railroad workers. Eddy offered $75,000 to start the hospital if the city would provide land for it. Citizens raised $4,000 needed to purchase a site on South Main. A frame building 300 feet long and two stories high was constructed. In 1885 the Sisters of Charity of the Incarnate Word were invited to take charge of nursing. Bishop N. A. Gallagher asked Mother St. Pierrette Cinquin, the mother superior of the order, to visit the hospital, where the chief surgeon persuaded her to send ten sisters to Fort Worth to staff it. Only a few months after the sisters arrived, on April 5, 1885, the hospital burned. The railroad rebuilt it and continued to operate it until 1889, when they sold the building to the sisters; they renamed it St. Joseph's Infirmary. In 1898 a new building (left) was completed. In 1930 its name was changed to St. Joseph Hospital. The Hospital Corporation of America bought the present building at 1401 South Main in 2002.

The 1950 Fort Worth city directory lists Clara Faye Deutschman with a profession of staff nurse. The nurse role of the 1950s differed dramatically from modern nursing. A thread from <u>allnurses.com</u> describes the profession Clara so proudly entered. "The nurses placed glass thermometers in specified cups containing isopropyl alcohol - red tops for the rectal and blue for the oral. Reusable needles and syringes required special sterilization and sharpening techniques. IV's came in glass bottles. Fathers waited in designated areas outside labor and delivery. Most physicians practiced general medicine. Nurses didn't routinely take blood pressures or perform patient assessments of lung and heart sounds in the 40s and early 50s, tasks considered part the practice of medicine. When ICU/CCU first came about nurses had to wait for the MD to come before giving anti-arrhythmic drugs. In many places, CRNA (nurse anesthetists) administered virtually all anesthesia agents as well as IV drugs."

After several years away from her West Texas roots, Clara returned to Abilene with an infant son, David Nadin. She spent most of her life as a divorced, single mother and worked most of her career at Hendrix Memorial Hospital.

Aunt Clara, like most nurses of her era, described the medical hierarchy. Doctors held a position of authority. She spoke of deferring to the physician in almost every detail of daily practice. When a physician walked onto the floor, the nurse stood and relinquished the chart and her chair to the doctor. No one questioned the physician. When the nurse recognized a need, she and her colleagues found a way to advocate for the patient. Often the nurse presented her suggestions for patient care in such a way that the doctor could accept them as his own ideas.

A normal occurrence in the hospital of the mid-twentieth century seems unthinkable today. The doctors and nurses thought nothing of smoking cigarettes in the nursing station as they documented patient care.

The nursing profession of the twenty first century scarcely resembles nursing of the 1940's. Aunt Clara proudly wore the distinctive uniform. A white dress (no pants for women) complete with white hosiery, freshly polished white shoes, a nursing cap, and the pin unique to the nurse's school identified mid-century nurses. Twenty-first century nurses prefer the comfort and flexibility of scrubs.

Depending on the role, nurses dress in business casual with or without a lab coat, sometimes identified only by nametags. Advanced practice nurses practice independently under the supervision of a physician. Like physicians, many nurses focus on specialty areas of medicine. A relaxed hierarchy promotes a team approach. Far from my grandfather's attitude about nursing as a subservient position bringing disgrace to his family, nursing represents a respected career. For the past decade, public surveys consistently place nurses at the top of the most trusted professions.

I often wonder what Aunt Clara would think of nurses today. I imagine her proudly cheering and championing the independent women and men who walk the path she so doggedly forged, encouraging them to uphold the values of a career we both loved.

Clara Faye Deutschman Nadin Garrett, R.N

Keeping things in perspective
1887 Nursing Job Description
scrubsmag.com/a-list-of-rules-for-nurses-from-1887/

In addition to caring for your 50 patients, each bedside nurse will follow these regulations:

1. Daily sweep and mop the floors of your ward, dust the patient's furniture and windowsills.

2. Maintain an even temperature in your ward by bringing in a scuttle of coal for the day's business.

3. Light is important to observe the patient's condition. Therefore, each day fill kerosene lamps, clean chimneys and trim wicks.

4. The nurse's notes are important in aiding your physician's work. Make your pens carefully; you may whittle nibs to your individual taste.

5. Each nurse on day duty will report every day at 7 a.m. and leave at 8 p.m., except on the Sabbath, on which day she will be off from 12 noon to 2 p.m.

6. Graduate nurses in good standing with the director of nurses will be given an evening off each week for courting purposes, or two evenings a week if you go regularly to church.

7. Each nurse should lay aside from each payday a goodly sum of her earnings for her benefits during her declining years, so that she will not become a burden. For example, if you earn $30 a month, you should set aside $15.

8. Any nurse who smokes, uses liquor in any form, gets her hair done at a beauty shop or frequents dance halls will give the director of nurses good reason to suspect her worth, intentions and integrity.

9. The nurse who performs her labors [and] serves her patients and doctors faithfully and without fault for a period of five years will be given an increase by the hospital administration of five cents per day

The Eve of the Day Everything Changed

Murrell Haskell Carr

"Yesterday, December 7, 1941 —
A date, which will live in infamy —
The United States of America was suddenly and deliberately
attacked by naval and air forces of the Empire of Japan."
President Franklin D. Roosevelt

Murrell Haskell Carr

The young soldier quickly packed the last of his personal belongings. Discharge papers on top, readily accessible. His buddies urged him, "Come on, Carr. You're wasting leave time. Let's get this party started."

One last night on the town – the lush beauty of the island offered a drastic contrast to the arid Texas family farm. The young soldier scarcely resembled the naïve teenager who joined the United States Army. Two years earlier, he left the family farm eagerly anticipating the world beyond his limited Texas existence. The beauty of Hawaii exceeded even his wildest dreams. He fulfilled his service obligation and eagerly anticipated the next phase of his life. The army experience changed him. Though barely out of his teens, he no longer felt like a boy but rather a man, ready to take on the world.

"Let's go see Boggie's new movie, *Maltese Falcon.* It just opened at the theater in town." one soldier suggested.

"Good idea. We can sure use two hours of looking at Mary Astor. She's easy on the eyes," the others agreed.

The suspenseful murder mystery allowed two hours of escape from the duties of the army and the uncertainty of the days ahead. They lost themselves in the story as Humphrey Bogart's slick character; the cold-hearted, tough Sam Spade skillfully manipulated the suspects and the femme fatale. Descending into the world of crime, Sam flirted with evil disguised as an attractive woman. At the last moment, he escaped evil's grasp by resisting the temptation to identify with the accomplices. Good wins over evil when Spade trusted his self-protective instincts and honored his commitment to protect society.

The young men imagined themselves as the hero – resisting temptation and being the champion who always won. No more daydreaming – reality weighed on the Murrell's mind. Tomorrow he'd board a plane and head back to Texas. He resolved to seek some other career route. Life on the family farm failed to charm him. His restless spirit longed to see more of the world than the small Texas community offered.

"Let's go to the beach," someone suggested.

"Yea, I'm not eager to visit my bunk." Carr agreed.

Realizing they might never return to Hawaii and unsure when or if they'd see each other again, the men decided to make the night last. The unit celebrated discharge from the Army and their last night on the island paradise. Perhaps they revisited sites of good times shared. Maybe they met up with other soldiers or some girls they knew. Possibly, they just sat on the beach and watched the waves roll onto the shore.

"I'm hungry – anybody else ready for breakfast? I'll buy," one of the guys offered.

They found a familiar spot with a friendly waitress and ordered a hearty breakfast. Well-fed and tired after the night of celebrating, the soon to be civilians headed back to their duty station. A few more hours, and they'd be in route home.

As they walked toward the barracks, chaos greeted them – Bombs burst all around them – Screams of "Pearl Harbor's under attack!"

Early Sunday morning, December 7, 1941, everything changed. Discharge orders cancelled, Murrell Carr spent another two years in the army. Life changed. Now the soldiers focused on fighting a defined enemy, the axis of evil – Japanese, Germans, and Italians. "They started this, but we'll finish it!" became the American troops' motto.

Fighting Men of World War II Taylor County Edition documents Murrell Haskell Carr's military service from 1939 – 1945. He survived battles at Pearl Harbor, New Guinea, and the Southwest Pacific for which he received four bronze stars.

> "The bronze star authorized by Executive Order 9419 on February 4, 1944, was awarded to a person in any branch of the military service who while serving in any capacity with the Armed Forces of the United States on or after December 7, 1941, shall have distinguished himself by heroic or meritorious achievement or service, not involving participation in aerial flight, in connection with military operations against an armed enemy."
> www.afpc.af.mil/library/factsheets/factsheet

Like most of the young men of his generation, Murrell Haskell Carr served his country proudly. He rarely talked about the war and likely bristled at the idea of war hero designation. He returned to America and worked hard to provide the American dream for his wife and daughter. I wonder if he ever thought of Pearl Harbor with a cascade of emotions – fear, survivor guilt, gratitude, rage – all motivating him to live life. The life spared by a scheduled leave and a spontaneous night of celebrating with his army buddies.

A navy photographer snapped this photograph of the Japanese attack on Pearl Harbor in Hawaii on December 7, 1941, just as the USS *Shaw* exploded. (80-G-16871) National Archives

Laughter at His Own Expense

Grady Olan Carr

"Mix a little foolishness with your prudence.
It's good to be silly at the right moment. "
Horace.

The truckers who knew him best called him Goosey Grady, or more commonly, Goose. An involuntary, reflexive response earned him a descriptive nickname. They often recounted a story of the day it backfired on them all.

"We all knew Goose couldn't control the reflexive motion. If you poked him in the ribs, he'd jump and punch or slap the person directly in front of him. It provided comic relief in the endless hours of waiting for our trucks to be loaded. The perpetrator never endangered himself, only the unfortunate soul standing in the path of Grady's right hand. One particular day, Goose filled his cup with steaming hot coffee. Distracted by conversation with another driver, he failed to sense the presence of a person sneaking up behind him."

The next few moments played out like a scene from a future television episode on *America's Funniest Home Videos*. "Goose jumped a foot in the air, and the cup sailed through space. A splash of coffee, followed by a right-handed slap across the face stunned the unsuspecting, innocent victim. The minor injury resulted in discipline of the guilty parties. The story became legendary among the Merchant's drivers and curtailed horseplay in the workplace for some time. "

From his early days on the farm, his family and friends recognized Grady's extraordinary sense of humor. He loved to play pranks. His reserved temperament disguised his mischievous nature. Unlike his loud, boisterous Carr relatives, Grady displayed a quiet demeanor. Perhaps he inherited the soft-spoken manner from his mother's more reserved Benningfield family. He mastered the ability to cover his tracks, so no one traced the originator of the practical jokes. His reticent manner allowed him to pull off celebrated pranks without suffering the consequences of his father's wrath.

One Sunday morning, Grady's sister confidently began the introduction of a selected hymn. An oddly dissonant sound filled the little sanctuary. She paused, horrified at the sound. Their father stopped the song service, calmly opened the piano, and removed several hymnals from the soundboard of the old instrument. The prankster never confessed and the music continued without further incident. Although church members never proved it, they suspected the youngest Carr son. Grady stifled guffaws and hid his pleasure at the well-executed caper. He pulled off another good one.

Grady embraced the role of jokester as a way to cope with the difficult circumstances of life. Like his brothers, he answered the call to military service. During World War II, he served his country with honor. Though records fail to provide evidence, one family member remembered hearing about the award of a purple heart. When he returned to Texas following the war, he pursued a career as a truck driver with Merchant's Freight Line. He valued time with his family and chose to drive in town instead of over the road, so that he could be at home each night with his wife and their two sons.

Though Grady enjoyed a good joke, he knew when and how to be serious. He exemplified the family values of loyalty and hard work. Like all true tricksters, he took great pleasure in planning and executing pranks. He understood the value of being able to be the brunt of a joke. Whether at the price of another's dignity, or at his own expense, Goose loved to laugh.

Did You Eat Yet?

Margaret Francis Deutschman Steiner Grimes

"Be ready with a good meal or a bed when it's needed. Why, some have extended hospitality to angels without even knowing it! "
Hebrews 13:2 The Message

"She's as wide as she is tall" words often used to described Aunt Margaret.

Margaret Grimes loved to cook. More than cooking, she loved to watch people enjoy the food she lovingly prepared. After dispensing hugs to arriving guests, the first words the rotund, apron clad woman spoke, "Did you eat yet?"

Aromas beaconed visitors directly to the kitchen. The tiny space, Aunt Margaret's domain, left little room for helpers. Guest's mouths watered as they anticipated decadent tastes. A feeding frenzy ensued each time the cook announced, "Dinner's ready."

The women stood back while the men served themselves. They piled plates high with fried chicken, mashed potatoes with gravy, fried okra, black-eyed peas, corn, and cornbread. Once the men sat at the table, the women and children filled their plates. Sounds of contented "mmmm's" accompanied by the groans of overfilled stomachs assured the cook that she again satisfied the appetites of the people around her table.

The 1930's in rural Texas taught Margaret and her siblings to live with the bare necessities of life. The seven siblings certainly knew how to exist without luxuries. They worked hard and often struggled to provide essentials. Margaret prepared meals to insure no one ever left her home unsatisfied. She always prepared more than enough. Having survived lean years, like Scarlet O'Hara the abundant table evidenced her unvoiced motto, "As God is my witness, I'll never be hungry again."

She perfected her craft. Every dish created in her kitchen delighted the taste buds. She loved to eat as much as she loved to cook. She steadily gained weight and hardly resembled the tiny woman of her youth.

Margaret and Homer Grimes never spoke of their early marriages. Margaret's son, Eugene, provided the only reference to Margaret's first husband, Frank Steiner. The Steiner name provided the only connection between father and son.

Homer's marriage to the fifteen-year old, Annie Galloway, lasted only a short time. Annie's parents vehemently opposed her marriage to the twenty two year old, Mr. Grimes, and encouraged her to seek an annulment. Ironically, Annie died in a car accident the month following her husband's second marriage.

When Homer married Margaret, he gained a bride and a four-year old son. Though he never legally adopted Gene, he raised him as his own son. The couple welcomed another son, Homer Loyd, Jr. Together they buried a stillborn son, Darrell.

Parenthood represented an important responsibility, and the young mother took the role seriously. Though her sons quickly grew taller than their five-foot tall mother, she commanded their respect. The object of discipline, a thick razor strap, hung visibly on a doorframe for easy access. She succeeded in her goal. Her strict discipline produced responsible, self-disciplined men.

If Margaret ever aspired to a career beyond her home and family, the secret remained guarded. She delighted in her home and in her children. Her legendary culinary skills gained recognition beyond the family to the community. Anyone who entered the Grimes home, found a warm, welcoming environment. A lady with the gift of hospitality greeted each guest at the door with a hug, followed by "Have you had anything to eat?"

Even if you just got up from the table, you couldn't resist a trip to the kitchen to sample comfort food. You always wound up at her table, hoping today's dessert might be everyone's favorite, Mississippi Mud.

Mississippi Fudge Cake

4 Eggs
2 Sticks of Oleo
2 Cups of Sugar
1½ Cups of Flour
1/3 cup of Cocoa
Pinch of salt
1½ Cup of Pecans
Melt oleo and cocoa together, pour into mixing bowl containing all the remaining ingredients except for nuts. Mix well. Add nuts. Bake in oblong pain 40-45 minutes at 350-degree oven. Remove from oven, spread marshmallows on top, return to oven and melt, don't brown. Then put icing on and cover until cool.

Icing:
1 Stick of oleo
1/3 Cup of cocoa
1½ box of powdered sugar
1/3 cup milk or cream
1-Teaspoon vanilla
1 Cup of Pecans
Smidgen of salt
Have frosting ready when cake is taken from oven.
Eat as much as you can!

Perfect Dolls

Mary John Carr Jones Moore

"I liked dolls as a child, but as an adult, I love them!
They represent the good in all of us and display the diversity beauty
of mankind. "
Gayle Wray

The vintage bride doll caught my eye as I toured the doll museum in Granbury, Texas. It bore similarities to the one of my childhood memory. "My Aunt Mary John kept a doll almost identical to this one," I drew my daughter's attention to the exhibit.

Mother's older sister yearned for a child. Years passed, and she never conceived. After ten years of marriage, she remained childless and desperately wanted a baby. Instead of focusing on her unfulfilled desire, she frequently borrowed her nieces and nephews. She lavished time, energy and gifts on each of us. I suspected she enjoyed playing with the toys she provided as much as she loved spending time with my siblings and me.

One bedroom housed more toys than I, or most of my friends, owned. She allowed us to play with specific things but clearly established hands off rules for the collectable dolls. One item particularly captivated me. Displayed prominently in the room, a toddler sized bride doll remained out of the reach of curious children's hands. The doll represented every little girl's dream – the perfect dress with a matching veil covering her stylishly coiffed hair.

I spent hours studying every detail of the miniature bride. However, something felt wrong– something about the face. With so much attention to detail, why would the maker give a bride the face of a child?

Like many children and adults, Mary John cherished the miniature human images. As early as the fifteenth century, ornately costumed lady dolls replicated popular fashion of the culture. Toy makers introduced the first baby doll around 1710. After 1860, American doll firms gained prominence and by 1930s provided the preferred brands. Innovative creations allowed the dolls to open and shut their eyes, drink water, and wet themselves. After World War II, the availability of vinyl plastic allowed mass production of creations with molded features.

The Deluxe Reading Company marketed dolls through supermarkets from 1955 to 1973. The *grocery store dolls* provided an inexpensive alternative to department store dolls, though they offered a similar quality. Deluxe Reading Betty, the Beautiful Bride, stood thirty inches tall. The package included everything required for the perfect wedding day except the groom. Bending arms and legs attached to her soft vinyl body. Washable saran hair allowed the owner to change Betty's hairstyle. A veil, lace gloves, simulated pearl tiara and necklace, and high heel shoes complimented the perfect white bridal gown. More accessories consisted of a descriptive plaque, blue wrist tag, and stain glass plaque. A 45 LP single recording of Bing Crosby's "Because" provided the final touch. Delighted pre-teen girls dreamed of their future wedding day and re-enacted many possible scenarios.

No one witnessed any wedding ceremonies for Mary John's bride doll. She simply occupied an honored place on the bureau, as she waited for her prince charming. Visiting nieces projected their dreams on the inanimate object from a distance and wondered about the creepy face of a child in an adult costume.

"I made Mom drive around in the station wagon to all the shopping centers to get the wedding dress - that was the best outfit, because it was the most expensive!"
Anonymous Young Girl,
Early 1960s

In contrast to her sister, my mother easily conceived. Her four children arrived within a decade. When Mom announced her fourth pregnancy, Aunt Mary John imagined the perfect solution. She and her husband approached my parents. They wanted to adopt two-year-old, Patty, who frequently spent time with them while Mother worked.

Mother and Daddy often struggled to provide financially for a large family. Aunt Mary John loved all her nieces and nephews, but her connection with Patty was special. The vivacious child loved freely. When the toddler entered the room, she brought joy and an enthusiasm for life. My aunt's heart ached when her sister refused to consider the possibility. No matter how difficult her circumstances, Mother never considered giving up any of her children.

Though Mary John never realized her dream of becoming a mother, she continued to pour into the lives of others. After her first husband died, she remarried and gained the family she desired. She obtained the privilege of spoiling her grandchildren without the responsibility of raising children. She lived the truth of an unknown author's joyful expression, "If I'd known grandchildren were so much fun, I'd have had them first."

Mary John, Margaret, Granny (center) Murrell, Wanda

A Tortured Soul
Is Anyone Beyond Redemption?
Fredrick Benjamin Deutschman

"I write about the power of trying, because I want to be okay with failing. I write about generosity because I battle selfishness. I write about joy because I know sorrow. I write about faith because I almost lost mine, and I know what it is to be broken and in need of redemption. I write about gratitude because I am thankful - for all of it."
Kristin Armstrong

The minister stood at the podium and faced the mourners. "No one who lived like Fred Deutschman can ever go to heaven."

The stunned mourners sat in motionless silence. They heard nothing past the stinging statement. *Really? What did he just say? Surely, he didn't say what I thought I heard. Even if he found no value in the man whose lifeless body lay in the casket, how could he be so cruel?*

The fractured family struggled to make sense of Fred's tortured life. No one denied the sins Fred committed. Each person recalled an imperfect relationship with the deceased. So many bad memories surfaced. Couldn't anyone find redemptive qualities in the tortured young man?

Mary – the second wife – endured so much abuse from this man. She ignored the signs – red flags warned her not to marry him. Handsome and arrogant, he bragged to her of his conquests before their marriage. During their marriage, he was indiscreet about his unfaithfulness. Fred felt no compulsion to repay debts to anyone – friends, family, merchants. He spent money as soon as he got it – mostly on alcohol and partying. Frequent tearful confessions accompanied promises to change.

Over the years he genuinely repented, trusted Christ, returned to church, and even felt called to the ministry. He wanted to preach, but as with every job, quickly disillusioned, he soon returned to habits of drinking and cheating. The final blow came when he left Mary for their teenage babysitter.

Mary remembered the good times, too. She recalled her wedding day. They married in her parent's home. Her mother worked diligently to prepare the home for the couple's special day. She remembered feeling like a properly beautiful bride and visualized herself in the sheer pink wedding dress. Her Aunt Mae crocheted a white hat with pink ribbon trim as a wedding gift. Fred planned every other detail of the ceremony; choosing the bridesmaid, his sister Mary John, and a childhood friend as his best man. His brother-in-law, George Dooly, a newly ordained minister, conducted the ceremony. The young bride vowed to love, honor and obey until death parted them. Despite her husband's failure to honor their vows, Mary kept her promise.

She desperately wanted to believe in the goodness and value of his life. She remembered the times he sought forgiveness and vowed to serve God. She smiled at the thought of one evening when they visited the Dooly home. Fred purchased a tape recorder to practice preaching. The young couples spoke and sang into the machine and howled with laughter as they played back the recording. As they slowed down the sound, George's deep bass voice and already slow Texas drawl produced a comical noise.

Despite all Fred's faults, Mary respected his position as the father of their son. She brought Fred III to say good-bye to his father and resolved life would be different for her son.

Accompanied by her children, Verna traveled to Arizona from Noodle, Texas to say goodbye to the son she never understood. When the minister pronounced damnation on her son's soul, a guttural wail escaped, releasing all the pent up emotions of her heart and soul. Conflicting feelings flooded her heart and mind. She regretted their last phone conversation as she recalled the angry words exchanged. Neither expected it to be the last time they spoke. She disapproved of her son's lifestyle and made no secret of her objections.

The grieving mother recalled scenes from her son's life. She smiled at the thought of rocking her innocent baby boy. *Where had things gone wrong? Had she been too strict? Was she too lenient?* Her mind drifted to the day Fred convinced her to sign the papers allowing him to join the military. She rationalized that perhaps the military's discipline might tame the teenager's wild streak. Military life and the war experience only accentuated his character defects. After his military service, he returned to the small farm community a troubled and rebellious young man.

She failed to understand what happened during his time in the navy. None of the returning soldiers or sailors spoke about war experiences. Her stepsons returned, found jobs, and built lives for their families. However, Fred, Jr. returned a different man from the boy who left the farm. Perhaps the head injury he sustained on the boat changed his personality. Maybe, he simply could not un-see the horrors of war.

His habit of excessive alcohol consumption mocked her intolerant teetotaler stance. She marveled at the resemblance between Fred and the father he'd never known. Fred, Jr. bore a remarkable resemblance to his father. Beyond physical similarities, the men shared a penchant for alcohol and drunken behavior, which resulted in fatal accidents for both father and son.

Though the Deutschman-Carr siblings shared a history, they found it difficult to comfort each other. Each one in their own way tried to support and love their wayward brother. Always on the move, he never settled down, or stayed in one place for very long. When efforts to help failed, each sibling grew impatient and cut off contact. As they pondered the pastor's remarks, each examined their relationship and recalled the last interaction with Fred.

What if I'd tried just one more time? Perhaps he'd still be alive, if I'd reached out and offered a place to come. He's gone, and I don't have another chance.

Heartache and self-doubt took a back seat to the anger they felt as they focused on the third wife – the person they suspected of causing their brother's premature death.

Charlotte – wife number three – and her two young sons sat in the front row. She felt the angry stares of Fred's family burning through the back of her head. In their hearts and minds, she murdered their son and brother.

The marriage never on solid ground floundered. They remained married but behaved as single adults, partying and dating without regard to the marriage vows. Charlotte's plan to reconcile the marriage backfired. She ended her recent affair and asked her former lover to assure Fred that he no longer intended to pursue the relationship. However, Fred was not convinced, and an altercation occurred.

According to the wife, a drunk and disorderly Fred stumbled, fell, and hit his head on a chair. When the police questioned Charlotte and her friend, the couple claimed no foul play. They assumed Fred passed out and would sleep it off. Several hours later when he remained out cold, they noticed blood coming from the back of his head. Too late, they called for help. Fred never regained consciousness and died at the hospital a few days later. The coroner ruled accidental death.

Here they gathered – unable to comfort each other – lost in individual thought – recalling painful interactions – searching for good memories to ease the pain of lost opportunities – doubting the truth of the minister's statement – knowing no one is beyond the redemptive work of Jesus Christ – relieved not to be the judge of Fred's tortured soul.

Striking it Rich

Garland Bradford Dooley (Dooly)

Poor and content is rich, and rich enough.
William Shakespeare

CASH FOR LIVE BABY SQUIRRELS! The sign near the door of Merkel's general store caught the young teen's attention. *I've been hunting squirrels all my life. I just have to figure out how to catch them instead of shooting them. I'm going to be rich!* His mind raced with options for the construction of a trap to contain and transport the furry rodents.

He hurried home, ran directly to the barn, and collected scraps of wood and chicken wire. He hastily fashioned a cage with a trap door and baited it with table scraps. The next morning, a commotion rewarded his efforts.

Careful to avoid the sharp claws and teeth of the angry little mammal, he placed the cage in the back of his dad's old truck and delivered it to the petting zoo owner.

"I can't imagine who'd be crazy enough to pet one of these creatures," he remarked as he collected the promised reward.

He pocketed a quarter and headed for the icehouse, where he purchased a block of ice for the family's icebox. The monetary reward provided a contribution to the family necessities and gave him sense of pride. For the first time in his young life, he realized the importance of money.

Trapping baby squirrels began a lifetime search for entrepreneurial opportunities. In the early years, he worked in the west Texas oilfields. Before Garland's twenty-first birthday, he provided for his teenaged bride, Ruth, and a new baby. Though his *day jobs* paid the bills, he often sought another route – something that offered more joy.

"Uranium is selling for a small fortune," the young men agreed. "If we can find and sell uranium, we'll be rich and never have to work again."

The young wives misgivings failed to dissuade their husbands' dreams. Garland and his friend, Red Allen, pooled their resources, purchased a Geiger counter, and left their young families to seek a fortune in North Dakota.

A silvery-white, heavy metal, uranium provided an abundant source of energy. During the early 1940s, the Manhattan Project and interest in nuclear weapons created a demand for the element. Initially, scientists and researchers planned to avoid nuclear proliferation by buying and controlling all sources of the rare element. However, uranium proved to be more plentiful than they anticipated. Discovery of large deposits of uranium throughout the world thwarted the United States' control of the nuclear power source.

After a month, the would-be miners gave up on the quest for uranium. Broke and disillusioned they returned to Texas.

Garland left the oilfield and settled into a steady nine-to-five routine job in Abilene where he worked for much of his adult life. He continued to pursue opportunities to work for himself – upholstering furniture, moving mobile homes, repairing lawn mowers, and serving as a handy man.

As the years passed, the normally industrious man looked forward to retirement. No longer encumbered by the time clock, he chose projects to fill his free hours. Too much leisure time left him bored and seeking meaningful work. His mother's words echoed in his head, "Idle hands are the devil's workshop."

I'm older now and there is much I can no longer physically do. Who's going to hire me, anyway? But, I'm still able to do a lot. I like people. I'm a hard worker. He took a mental inventory of his attributes.

The available opportunities surprised the retiree. He secured a job sacking groceries at the local HEB and served students in the university cafeteria. More than supplementing his social security income, his job at Hardin Simmons University allowed him a social outlet. He enjoyed spending time with the college students. He chatted with them about anything from their weekend plans to their career goals.

Throughout his life, Garland put the needs of his family before the pursuit of a business of his own. He provided for them, sometimes working multiple jobs. If he regretted life choices, he never verbalized any disappointment. Instead, he found contentment in a job well done.

As he listened to the college students, perhaps he recalled the dreams and plans of his youth. He remembered the sense of accomplishment, as he successfully carried out his first business transaction. *Boy, I wish I'd caught a lot more squirrels.*

Childhood Perspectives of Life on the Farm

"I adored my Grandparents and have so many memories of that fine old white two story farm house sitting back among two maple trees. Lots of flowers, a big garden, large apple orchard. I loved the woods... so many paths and exciting things to do and discover. Large grape vines, plenty of nut trees and just a good place to be alone to wander around and explore. My sisters and I had a great imagination and we put it to use! Where big trees had been uprooted by storms, we said that was Indian burying ground and we did not dare disturb them."

Adine Cathey
September 8, 2008

The Art of Coffee

"I'm drinking from my saucer, cause my cup has overflowed"
Gospel Song Lyrics – John Paul Moore

"You better not drink that coffee. It'll turn your toes black," Granddaddy often quipped to his grandchildren.

Long before coffee shops added variety to the caffeine loaded drink, Granddaddy created a perfect concoction. Each morning started with a trip to the barn to milk the cows. A slamming screen door signaled his return to the kitchen. His presence filled the entire house. The floor shook under his weight. He never concerned himself with sleeping guests. He awoke before sunrise and lived by the philosophy of not burning daylight. If he was awake, the rest of the household should be as well. He worked hard and expected the same of everyone in the home.

While Granddaddy milked the cows, Granny started breakfast and placed the coffee pot on the stove to brew. A hearty breakfast fueled the family for a hard day's work.

As he opened the back door, he announced in a booming voice that matched his size, "Breakfast."

I bolted from the bed, pulled on my clothes and took my place at the kitchen table. Granddaddy commanded respect without the need for physical discipline. I instinctively understood the expectation – no dawdling or laziness. I loved the simple pleasures of spending time at my grandparent's farm. Sleeping later meant wasting precious time. I never considered missing the morning ritual.

The experienced farmer carefully skimmed cream from the top of the milking pail and placed it in a small Marshall Pottery crock pitcher. He poured the remainder of the milk into the larger matching crock and placed it in the refrigerator to cool.

Granddaddy took his place at the head of the table and proceeded to prepare his cup of coffee. His coffee cup sat in a large saucer, which more accurately resembled a bowl. He poured coffee into the cup, leaving a large amount of room for cream and sugar. He carefully stirred the tan liquid, adding cream until the color met his specifications. Then he carefully poured the concoction into the deep saucer, slowly breathed in to savor the aroma, blew across the top to cool it slightly. Finally, he lifted the saucer to his lips and took the first slurp. The process continued until he drained the saucer, enjoying ever drop.

I never saw anyone enjoy coffee as much as my grandfather did. He never rushed the preparation He enjoyed the process as much as the flavor. The simple pleasure of drinking from a saucer started the day on a positive note.

As a little girl, I believed anything my Granddaddy Carr told me. It never occurred to me to ask if his toes turned black, since he drank coffee every morning. I longed to experience the pleasure coffee provided, dared to tempt fate, and begged to sample the warm liquid.

Most mornings I gulp down my coffee to get the caffeine rush. However, sometimes on quiet mornings at home I really enjoy a good cup of coffee. I recall the sweet country mornings spent drinking coffee with Granddaddy. I still add cream and sweetener, take in the aroma, and blow across the top of the cup, before finally lifting it to my lips to take the first sip. I don't slurp – maybe I should. Perhaps, I should pour the sweet tan liquid in a saucer to remind me of the blessings of life's simple joys, like having a perfect cup of coffee.

Modern Conveniences

"Acting is not an important job in the scheme of things. Plumbing is."
Spencer Tracy

"Mom, I really have to go to the bathroom. Pleeease, go with me! I'm scared," I pleaded.

"Stop being such a baby. There's nothing to be afraid of," Mother displayed her normal lack of tolerance for whining.

Finally, the urgency overcame my sense of dread. I trekked out the back door, through the backyard gate, and followed the trail to the outhouse. I darted past the chicken house and the hog pen.

The warm slop emitted an unpleasant smell. However, the stench of the pigpen paled when compared to the disgusting odor from the outhouse. The tiny structure served one purpose – bodily elimination. Though the bench had two rounded holes, only one person at a time ever occupied the outhouse.

The recognizable style provided an open space at the top to allow ventilation and light while preserving individual privacy. During the early nineteenth century, carved crescent moons and stars appeared on the door of outhouses. While the carvings allowed additional light and ventilation, it served to delineate users of the facility. A moon and star together represented a unisex outhouse, while a star alone indicated a men's privy. The outhouse adorned with a moon alone was reserved for the ladies.

If carvings decorated my grandparent's outhouse, no one paid attention to what they represented. A single two-holed structure served the entire extended family.

Though the stench assaulted my senses, I feared the outhouse for an entirely different reason. Each time I entered the building I peered into each of the holes before sitting down. Assured no snakes hid in the darkness, coiled and ready to strike my bare behind, I proceeded to do my business.

The old farmhouse lacked modern conveniences. They managed without indoor plumbing and running water. Granny was content with a wringer washing machine that agitated the clothes. She ran each item through the ringer before placing them in a basket, carried them to across the yard, and hung them on the clothesline. She celebrated when Daddy and Granddaddy figured out how to pump water from the well to the kitchen sink.

"I really, really hate that outhouse. It stinks. Why don't Granny and Granddaddy have a bathroom? " I asked my parents as we returned home after a weekend visit.

"They really should. They're getting older. A bathroom would make life a lot easier. It is 1958 - long past time for indoor plumbing at the farm. While we're adding a bathroom, they could use a washer and dryer," Daddy told mother on the drive from Noodle to Abilene.

His confidence bolstered by a newly issued plumbing license, he continued, "If your dad and Buddy will help me, I can install indoor plumbing. It should only take a few weekends."

The men in our family possessed a natural ability to solve complex construction and mechanical issues. The materials represented a significant cost, but Granddaddy eagerly agreed to finance the modernization of the old farmhouse.

Everyone excitedly watched the progress. My grandparents rarely expressed emotions, but they enthusiastically anticipated the improvements. Granny and her daughters cooked hearty meals, so the men could keep on working.

"Okay, Verna, we're done. Come, try it out," Daddy announced in his characteristic Texas drawl.

Appropriately, Granny initiated the laundry, toilet, and bathtub. "I'm a lady of leisure with that new washer and dryer, but I think I'll still hang out the laundry – I like the way the sheets smell when I take them off the line. So nice! – The bath felt really good," she voiced her final approval.

The modern conveniences pleased Granny and Granddaddy. However, their oldest granddaughter was the most delighted of all! Never again would I trek down the well-worn path to the outhouse.

An occasional weekend camping trip or port-a-potties at an outdoor concert venue reminds me of the trek to the old outhouse. When the odor assaults my senses, I vow never to take indoor plumbing for granted.

Not so very long ago, the family farmhouse lacked such amenities.

Don't Answer the Phone – It's Not Our Ring

"An amazing invention but who would ever want to use one?"
US President Rutherford B. Hayes, 1876

Two short rings broke the silence in the farmhouse. I darted to answer the phone. "Don't answer it! That's not our ring."

Puzzled I paused, "Not our ring?"

The insistent ringing of the phone eventually stopped. "That's the neighbor's ring." Granny explained.

By the end of the week, I learned to distinguish the distinctive signals that came from the black rotary phone. Two short rings belonged to one neighbor, two longs to another, long-short to even another, and a short-long signified the call was for my grandparents.

Party lines were common in mid-twentieth century rural Texas. During World War II, the party lines provided the only option for telephone communication. Once available, few families in remote communities could afford a private line. For my frugal, depression era grandparents the luxury of a private phone line seemed wasteful.

Finances dictated the length of phone conversations. Since none of their children lived locally, calls from anyone except neighbors required long distance charges. Infrequent calls and brief conversations saved money. The neighbors showed respect for each other by keeping conversations brief.

Though party line members demonstrated consideration for the privacy of their friends, there was no expectation of privacy. Anyone on the shared line might pick up the phone at any moment and hear personal conversations. Callers guarded every word, careful not to share any information they didn't want the entire community to know.

Telephones provided urgent communication – facts without personal commentary. Face-to-face visits provided the best opportunity for private conversations. Hand written letters conveyed information as well as emotions. Long letters discussed details of daily life, shared the news of the community, and expressed emotions.

Half-century later technologic advances revolutionize communication. The internet and cell service supplement landlines. Many customers rely on cellular service for all phone communication and eliminate the need for long distance carrier. E-mail and text messages make hand written letters almost obsolete. Cell phones and the internet make the world a much smaller place, allowing immediate communication with anyone who connects to the internet.

The magic of Skype or Facetime allows direct connection and personal communication over the world. Communication occurs hundreds or thousands of miles away.

We pay a price for the amazing, wonderful opportunities technology affords. Text messages provide instant access but fail to produce the excitement of receiving a letter – of eagerly waiting for the postman to deliver a letter from someone special. Nothing compares to the experience of holding a letter, seeing the familiar handwriting, reading and re-reading each carefully crafted word.

Despite technology's advances, it lacks the personal touch. Hand written cards and letters represent sweet expressions of thoughtfulness. Virtual hugs and kisses are nice but can never replace the real thing!

Watching the World Turn

"Soap operas got nothing on my family history."
Kiersten White

Lunch provided the largest meal of the day at the farmhouse. Granddaddy started each morning by milking the cows. Immediately after breakfast, he climbed on a John Deer tractor and spent most mornings plowing and completing farm chores.

The rigorous farm routine resembled the most structured business schedule. Farm laborers raced to complete intensive work before the Texas sun generated unbearable heat making continued work impractical if not dangerous. By noon, the men retreated to the farmhouse and the daily lunch feast. The midday meal included meat and potatoes as well as vegetables from the garden. The substantial nutrition provided the energy needed to complete afternoon tasks.

The noontime ritual consisted of a blessing of the food, followed by eating the delicious fare. With his belly full, Granddaddy pushed his chair back and announced, "Time to go watch the world turn."

The television occupied a corner in the front room. The large open fan (swamp cooler) filled the window space at the north end of the room and provided the only cool air in the house. He stretched out on the sofa and prepared to lose himself in a fantasy soap opera world.

As a spinning globe settled into position, the musical theme signaled the start of the iconic soap opera. *As the World Turns* premiered on April 2, 1956 and ran for fifty-four years. It remained the last soap opera produced by Proctor and Gamble and aired the last episode on September 18, 2009.

As the World Turns creator, Irna Phillips, distinguished herself as a writer of radio soap operas. The half-hour television format allowed her to develop characters and explore psychological realism. She placed professional characters at the center of the story line. Phillips wrote, "As the world turns, we know the bleakness of winter, the promise of spring, the fullness of summer, and the harvest of autumn – the cycle of life is complete."

Each day viewers tuned in to see what new challenge confronted the fictional characters. The average life of the audience contrasted sharply with the charmed life of the educated professionals on the small screen. The small Mid-Western lifestyle bore few similarities to the harsh reality of the rural Texas farm. The storyline presented one problem after another, and ordinary people escaped their own lives and focused on the needs of a fantasy world.

As the World Turns allowed my grandparents a break from real-life challenges if only for a few minutes a day. Perhaps they drew comfort from rationalizing. At least we don't have as many problems as the characters on *As the World Turns.*

In reality, no soap opera drama rivaled the challenges of their real lives. Their true stories supplied intriguing themes. However, the primary personalities chose to keep events of their past lives private, leaving their heirs to speculate and romanticize. Their real life stories equal the drama of any possible fictional tale.

Don't Buy This Machine

"Sewing mends the soul."
Author Unknown

The sewing machine decorating a corner of my bedroom scarcely resembles the one I remember from my childhood. Stripped and restored, it looks more like the one advertised in Montgomery Ward and Company's catalogue number 82 of 1913. Although Montgomery Ward warranted the machine for five years, replacing all defective parts free of charge, marketers encouraged catalogue shoppers to purchase the more expensive, more durable unit.

In 1913, a new Oakland model treadle sewing machine retailed for $8.75. For an additional $1.25, the customer received the additional set of attachments. A portable, toy model "The Juvenile" priced at $2.95 provided the only less expensive option.

THE OAK-LAND $8.75

HERE IS A SEWING-MACHINE WE DO NOT RECOMMEND

While we warrant this sewing machine for 5 years, and will replace any defective parts free of charge during this period, we do not recommend the Oakland. Under all circumstances you are advised, if possible, to order one of our better grades—the Damascus 3LF180, for example.

The sewing head of the Oakland is substantially built. It is enameled in black, and decorated with gold colors. The automatic bobbin-winder is of the same mechanical construction as on our higher priced sewing machines.

The stand is made of round iron, well finished, in black enamel. The woodwork is finished in oak. There are five drawers. The machine is fitted with drop-head, self-setting needle and self-threading shuttle. Oakland Sewing machine, as illustrated and described. On cars at factory, northern Illinois. Shipping weight, 120 lbs.

3LF2010—Price $8.75
3LF2012—Oakland Sewing Machine, as described and illustrated above, with a complete set of Griest attachments.
Price $9.50

At some time in its history, someone, probably my little grandmother, painted the cabinet with several thick coats of burgundy paint. The deep burgundy imitated the dark cherry wood adorning the more stylish homes of the day. When my Momo died, I inherited the machine. For years, it sat in the corner of my living room with the same crocheted piece protecting the top of the cabinet exactly as I remembered it in my grandmother's home. I planned to have it restored one day but never made the project a priority. My husband seized an opportunity to fulfill my *one-of-these day's* task. I pictured Momo's disapproval as her prized possession temporarily relocated to the woodshop class in the prison where my husband taught. Imagine my surprise when the refurbished cabinet revealed tiger oak wood hidden below the layers of burgundy paint. A true treasure disguised by a poor effort to imitate a wealthier look.

No identifying marks document the manufacturing year of Momo Dooly's sewing machine. Any lettering or markings on the machine itself wore away long ago. The cabinet drawers still hold the original attachments complete with the small oil can used to keep all moving parts in good working order. Perhaps a neighbor or friend presented the young woman with the machine when she upgraded her own. Maybe she purchased a used model from someone in the community. Possibly, she inherited the machine when she assumed the care of her aging mother.

As a teenager and even later as a young mother and wife of a sharecropper, a $10 purchase represented a major expenditure. The appliance provided a means to clothe the family. Momo owned few ready-made dresses, a luxury beyond her meager means. She constructed dresses and aprons for herself and shirts for her boys from flour sacks often without benefit of a pattern. Unlike other modern conveniences, the family considered the sewing machine a necessary tool.

The old treadle sewing machine embodied more than an essential appliance. Momo owned very few material possessions. She treasured this piece of furniture. It belonged to her and no one else used it. Seated at the sewing machine, she escaped the reality of a difficult life. Her feet and legs pumped faster and faster, making the needle fly. As she worked, strains of "My Bonnie Lies over the Ocean" or "I'll Fly Away" accompanied the rhythm of her work. Sewing transported her to another place – a place free of stress and grief – a place filled with acceptance and love.

Montgomery Ward's marketers encouraged customers to buy a more substantial model. Though the machine failed to meet the company's standards, they underestimated its importance to one sharecropper's wife. Over one hundred years later, it remains an integral part of our family history – memories of Momo singing and sewing – priceless.

Fish Stories – No Bones About it

"The solution to any problem – work, love, money, whatever – is to go fishing, and the worse the problem, the longer the trip should be."
John Gierach

"I got one!" I yelled excitedly.

"That's a Jonah fish," Granddaddy observed.

"Jonah fish?" I played along. No matter how often I heard the story, I never tired of the game. "What's a Jonah fish?"

"It's not the fish that swallowed Jonah. It's the fish that Jonah swallowed on the way to the belly of the whale."

Granddaddy valued the experience of taking his grandchildren fishing. He intentionally planned the trip to show us how to catch fish. Each fishing trip required careful preparation. Before we left the farm, we filled the bait can with scoops of the moist earth containing the wiggling worms. Granny packed a lunch of sandwiches and fruit. We left immediately after breakfast and returned just before dinner.

My favorite fishing trips occurred when my cousin, Jo Ann, visited from Dallas. The same city girls who delighted in digging in the mud for worms an hour earlier squeamishly shied away from baiting our own hooks. Granddaddy patiently threaded the worms on our hooks. When we successfully caught a fish, he removed it from the line and placed each new catch on a stringer. The only catch and release program involved the ones Jonah swallowed. The fish, if deemed big enough to keep, eventually found its way to the frying pan. More than a sport, fishing provided a food source.

Not everything we caught wound up on the dinner table. While Granny Carr loved fishing, she left the instruction to Granddaddy. While he busied himself with assisting the children, she baited her own hook and cast her line in the river. When her cork bobbed, she forcefully jerked the pole to set her hook. The force of her pull propelled an object from the river through the air. Unfortunately, the hook failed to set, and the creature landed in Granny's apron-clad lap. Something in Granny's voice caught the attention of everyone in hearing distance. "John, come here. I need you," her voice conveyed the urgency of the situation.

"Use your apron to fling it away from you, he calmly instructed.

Granny jumped to her feet, shook her apron, flinging the snake as far away from her body as possible. Granddaddy moved swiftly and cut off the snake's head. With the threat neutralized, we returned to our fishing mission until the stringer held enough fish to feed the family.

Granddaddy consulted the Farmer's Almanac before embarking on fishing expeditions. The Farmer's Almanac based its recommendation on the moon's phase and zodiac sign. The calendar provided a forecast of the best days to expect a successful catch. More often than not, the prediction proved correct. We rarely failed to catch enough for a fish fry.

One family outing stands out in my memory when our entire family went to the river. Noodle Creek with its tree-lined banks flowed through the farmland of a nearby neighbor. The stream joined other tributaries to form the Clear Fork of the Brazos River, which ran thirty-seven miles through several counties including Jones, east of Snyder, Texas and eventually joined the Brazos River at its mouth near South Bend.

The creek's water level depended on the amount of recent rainfall. Most days it barely trickled over the creek bed. Recent rains caused the creek to flow swiftly and swell to waist high depths. Deeper waters and a positive almanac forecast promised a successful outcome.

Our normal fishing equipment consisted of a cane pole, line, cork, and stringer. I watched as Granddaddy, Daddy and my uncle prepared for a dramatically different kind of fishing expedition. They spread a seine net on the bank and got ready to enter the creek.

The seine fishing technique employs a net weighted on the bottom and buoyed on the top with floats. Generations passed down the method of harvesting fish. Native American Indians wove nets from roots and wild grasses and attached cedar floats. Stone-age anglers employed similar methods.

Daddy and Uncle Buddy carried the net into the water. They waded several hundred feet and emerged from the stream with a net filled with fish. They repeated the process until they caught enough fish to feed the extended family. The task completed, we packed up, returned to Granny and Granddaddy's farm. The men cleaned the fish and turned them over to the women for a Texas sized fish fry.

It required a feast to satisfy the hearty appetites of the assembled crowd. Anytime the Carr siblings and their families gathered, the scene resembled a family reunion. The women knew how to cook for a crowd. Platters heaped high with fried fish and fried potatoes lined the buffet. Sliced tomatoes, fresh peas, and other vegetables from Granny's garden filled large serving dishes. Cornbread accompanied every special meal, and a variety of desserts completed the menu.

"Dinner's ready," Granny finally announced.

"Bless the food, so we can eat before it gets cold," she instructed.

The family gathered around the table as instructed. Daddy blessed the food. The brief prayer always ended with the phrase, "Bless this food to the nourishment of our bodies. Amen."

Each person eagerly waited for the "Amen" which signaled the beginning of a feeding frenzy.

Granddaddy assumed his position at the head of the table and began flaking small bits of fish from the bones. He carefully rubbed each piece between his index and middle fingers and his thumb, feeling for any small bones that might stick in his grandchildren's throat or cause them to choke. He continued his chore and served each child before finally preparing his own plate and eating his fill of fish.

Fishing with my grandparents provided life lessons. Granddaddy used examples in nature to share the story of Jonah, so I retained it for a lifetime. He modeled love by simple acts of service.

I loved fishing. I loved eating fried catfish. Most of all I loved spending time with my Granddaddy.

A bad day fishing is better than a good day at work.
Author Unknown

Frozen Seats for Frozen Treats

"There's nothing wrong with me a little ice cream won't fix."
Author Unknown

"Come sit on this bucket."

Each cousin took turns sitting on the hand-crank freezer while one of the men turned the crank. When our frozen rear-ends needed relief, another cousin took a turn. Although I never fully understood the necessity of this practice, I never declined when instructed to take my turn. We took the responsibility quite seriously. If I failed to take my turn, I might forfeit my bowl of ice cream. Unwilling to take that chance, I weighted down the freezer. Otherwise, the wooden bucket twisted making the task of turning the crank more difficult.

Perhaps having us take a seat on the ice cream freezer kept us from pestering the adults with constant questioning of "Is it ready yet?"

The women remained in the house busy with meal preparation, while the men gathered in the back yard. When one tired of turning the crank, another would take his place. The process continued until the frozen concoction firmed, and the handle no longer moved. They tested the firmness by each trying to turn it once someone declared, "I think it's ready."

Then they packed it in ice and covered the top layer of ice with rock salt. It set while we ate dinner. After dinner, we took our bowls and anxiously waited to receive our portion, the reward for a frozen butt.

Hot Texas summer days called for something cold. Non-discriminating tastes knew only that it tasted yummy. No one offered a critique on the technique or the flavor. We simply devoured the scrumptious sweet ice cream.

Commercially produced ice cream suffices and satisfies the basic craving for a favorite dessert. The fresh ingredients of homemade ice cream create a unique taste not found in the mass produced carton.

Homemade ice cream requires time and planning. The process requires patience and reinforces the value of waiting for good things. One taste of the sweet, ice-cold cream transports me to a time long ago, when obeying the command to sit on a bucket of ice resulted in a delectable treat.

Good things come to those who wait.

The History of Ice Cream
Source: The 2004 Old Farmer'sAlmanac

The **history of ice cream** is a messy one. Many nations claim to have **invented** it, just as various individuals take credit for it. Even if its origin remains murkey, it makes for a chilling drama! If you are searching for the answer to "Who invented ice cream?" that's a trick question. There isn't just one single person! Read on ...

A.D 54–68: For centuries, iced desserts were a luxury. Roman Emperor Nero is said to have sent his slaves into the mountains to fetch snow to mix with nectar, fruit pulp, and honey, although this widely told tale may be a myth.

A.D. 618–907: The origins of ice cream date back to China's T'ang period, probably as a dish for the country's rulers. The founder of the dynasty, King T'ang of Shang, kept 94 "ice men" on hand to lug ice to the palace to make a dish made of koumiss (heated, fermented milk), flour, and camphor.

1744: American colonists brought along recipes from Europe. On May 19, 1744, a group of VIP's dined at the home of Maryland Governor Thomas Bladen. Present was a Scottish colonist who described "a Dessert...Among the Rarities of which is was Compos'd, was some fine Ice Cream which, with the Strawberries and Milk, eat most deliciously." This is the first written account of ice cream consumption in the new colonies.

1782: Ever hear how Martha Washington left a bowl of sweet cream on the back steps of Mount Vernon one night, and the next morning discovered ice cream? Nice story, but not true. George Washington did have, described in his ledger, "a cream machine for ice."

1843: Until September 9, 1843, ice cream was made by the "pot freezer method," but on this day, Nancy M. Johnson of Philadelphia got her "artificial freezer" patented, containing a tub, cylinder, lid, dasher, and crank. This design is still widely used today.

1851: Baltimore dairyman Jacob Fussell opened the first commercial ice cream factory. He had a surplus of cream—so he built an ice cream factory in Seven Valleys, Pennsylvania, and shipped it to Baltimore by train. Business boomed, and Fussell became the father of the wholesale ice cream industry.

1880: Buffalo, NY; Evanston, IL; Two Rivers, WI; and Ithaca, NY all claim to have invented the ice cream sundae. Wherever it happened, it first started appearing in soda fountains during the 1880's. It was invented because ice cream sodas weren't allowed to be sold on Sundays; the ice cream sundae was a way to circumvent that restriction. On September 22, 1903, there is a recorded application for a patent for the ice cream cone by Italo Marchiony.

1939: Grocery stores didn't start selling ice cream until the 1930's, and by WWII, ice cream had become so popular that it turned into somewhat of an American symbol (Mussolini banned it in Italy for that same reason). Ice cream was great for troop morale, and in 1943, the U.S. Armed Forces were the world's largest ice cream manufacturers!

Whatever the history, ice cream is here to stay!

My Favorite Homemade Ice Cream Recipe

Separate 6 eggs

Beat egg white until stiff

Beat egg yolk until thick and lemon yellow

Fold egg yolks into egg whites

Fold in one can of sweetened condensed milk

Add sugar if added sweetness is desired (I use about ½ cup)

Add 1-Tablespoon vanilla (or to taste)

At this point, you can add additional fruit or flavorings as desired

Pour mixture into ice cream freezer canister. Add milk to fill line

Add ice around the canister along with rock salt

Follow manufacturer's direction for freezing with your machine

Savor the flavor!

Exploring a Cowgirl Career

Cows are amongst the gentlest of breathing creatures; none show more passionate tenderness to their young when deprived of them; and, in short, I am not ashamed to profess a deep love for these quiet creatures.

Thomas de Quincey

"Sulk – Sulk – Sulk," the gentle animals recognized Granddaddy's distinctive voice.

Daily it beckoned them from the field. They nudged each other until each cow occupied a place at the trough.

Every day of our visit to the farm my cousin, Jo, and I participated in the daily ritual. We pleaded, "Can we ride them?"

The farm provided a home to a variety of animals. Dogs, cats, and chickens roamed freely. Pigs wallowed in a muddy pen away from the other animals. Cows grazed in the fields until called to the safety of the feeding lot. A saddle hung from the rafters of one of the out buildings.

My curiosity prompted me, "Mom, we found a saddle in the shed today. Did Granddaddy own a horse?"

"When Mary John and I were girls, we had a horse. I never liked riding horses that much, but Mary John and Granddaddy rode. One day while herding cattle, the horse bucked and threw Granddaddy. By sunset, Granddaddy found a new home for the horse. He wouldn't take the chance of one of his family getting hurt. I never understood why he kept that saddle."

After a week of our pleas, Granddaddy acquiesced. He fashioned a bridle from a rope to assure he could control the calf. He chose the gentlest calf from the herd. Carefully, he lifted each granddaughter onto the back of the little calf. My grandfather led the calf around the fenced lot allowing each child a chance to ride. A reticent Jo changed her mind and politely declined.

Two years separated my younger sisters, who grew up much like twins. They shared every life experience. This picture of the afternoon on the farm speaks volumes. My sisters sat together on the back of the calf. Granddaddy tightly held the rope and assumed a protective stance. Lisa studied the calf, while Patty gazed lovingly at the man all of his granddaughters adored.

Granddaddy and his cowgirl

Jo watched each of us take a turn. Her confidence boosted by the bravery of her young cousins. "If the babies can ride her, I can at least pet her. But, I'm not standing behind her. She might be like a horse and kick me," she rationalized and approached the animal from the side.

The fun ended abruptly, when without warning, the calf landed a firm sideways kick to Jo's thigh propelling the girl across the lot. The horrified adults rushed to take care of the injured child.

The short-lived cowgirl career ended after one brief afternoon. No Carr granddaughter ever rode another cow, or calf for that matter.

Saturday at the Five and Dime

Pick my left pocket of its silver dime, but spare the right —
it holds my golden time!
Oliver Wendell Holmes

"We're going to town tomorrow. You'll need to dress and be ready to go early. I want to be first in line at the doctor's office," Granddaddy announced.

Dr. Sadler's office operated on a first come first serve basis. If the patient signed in early, he avoided a long wait. It never occurred to me to ask what ailment necessitated the visit. My grandparent's private nature kept such matters closely guarded.

Time away from the farm required careful planning. Not one to waste a trip to town, Granddaddy considered every detail carefully. He loaded the car with everything that needed attention. Tomorrow's visit to Merkel would begin with a visit to the doctor's office, proceed to the welding shop, then to feed store, followed by a stop at Ben Franklin, and finally conclude at Carson's Supermarket.

Verna inventoried the pantry and listed the staples she needed from the grocery store. The family grew fruits and vegetables, and raised chicken, beef, and pork. They purchased the things they couldn't produce. She considered what she needed from Ben Franklin. She planned to purchase pink embroidery thread for a set of pillowcases, some crochet thread for her handwork, and some material to patch the hole in John's work overalls. She contemplated the day. *I hope we have time to look around at all the pretty things they have on the shelves. It will entertain the girls. They really enjoy looking at all the toys. Looking doesn't cost anything.*

Running the farm required attention seven days a week. The essential chores included feeding the animals, milking the cows, and gathering eggs. A trip to town meant being away from the duties of the farm for the better part of the day. The scarce supply and high price of gasoline encouraged residents to make every trip count. Neighbors helped each other. A brief call announced, "We're going to town in the morning. Can you keep an eye on things? Do you need anything from town?"

We rose early Saturday morning and ate breakfast. I helped Granny with the dishes while Granddaddy tended to the animals. We piled into the old Chevy and embarked on our adventure. "Roll down the windows. It activates my air conditioning." Granddaddy instructed.

"Wow! When did you get air in your car?" I responded enthusiastically.

"I have two fifty air conditioning. Two windows down and 50 miles an hour." He laughed heartily at his own joke and my naivety.

We entertained ourselves by sharing stories and singing familiar tunes until we reached our destination. I waited anxiously as we completed one errand and then another. My favorite stop would be the last one. I loved Merkel's local five and dime store. Its location next to Carson's Supermarket allowed me to look around while my grandparents bought groceries. I browsed the aisles that contained personal and household items. I gazed longingly at toys, games, and even cosmetics.

In the nineteenth century, rural residents commonly ordered necessities from Sears Roebuck or Montgomery Ward catalogues. Others bought items from dry goods stores. Clerks at these stores stood behind the counters, fetched merchandise, and priced it at the owner's whim. In 1879, small town life changed when Frank W. Woolworth introduced a new way to shop. He marketed nickel-priced items on self-serve tables. For decades, Americans frequented Woolworth's and other similar variety stores.

The Hammond family owned the Ben Franklin Five and Dime in Merkel. It offered a wide variety of items at affordable prices. On any given day, customers found cosmetics and perfumes as well as cast-iron skillets.

Dooly Siblings at Dooley's in Fredricksburg

Children discovered toys – jacks, marbles, toy soldiers, and paper dolls. Merchandise filled each bin and every shelf. Larger items sat on the floor.

Many years later, my siblings and I visited Fredricksburg, Texas. A delighted quartet posed in front of Dooley's 5-10 & 25 Cent store. Imagine our delight to meet the owner of the store. We sought out the owner who shared the history of the business. His grandfather Charles purchased the store after World War I, John Dooley (who shares my paternal grandfather's name with a variation of the spelling Dooly) inherited the business and passed it down to his son, Tim.

The visit to Dooley's provided a nostalgic stroll through my memories. Each of us eagerly called attention to one item after another – things we recalled using during childhood but hadn't thought of in years. I couldn't resist the temptation to purchase a package of plastic cowboys and Indians for my younger brother. He bought a quite handy kitchen tool for each of us. The unique pickle picker serves to remind me of a pleasant day with my siblings and many happy memories of days spent with Granny and Granddaddy at the local five-n-dime.

It's not what you look at that matters, it's what you see.
Henry David Thoreau

Nothing Interrupts Gunsmoke

"Good evening. My name's Wayne. Some of you may have seen me before; I hope so. I've been kicking around Hollywood a long time. I've made a lot of pictures out here, all kinds, and some of them have been Westerns. And that's what I'm here to tell you about tonight: a Western—a new TV show called Gunsmoke. No, I'm not in it. I wish I were, though, because I think it's the best thing of its kind that's come along, and I hope you'll agree with me; it's honest, it's adult, it's realistic. When I first heard about the show Gunsmoke, I knew there was only one man to play in it: James Arness, who is actually my friend. He's a young fellow, and maybe new to some of you, but I've worked with him and I predict he'll be a big star. So you might as well get used to him, like you've had to get used to me! And now I'm proud to present my friend,
Jim Arness in Gunsmoke. "
John Wayne, first Gunsmoke TV episode, "Matt Gets It."

"Be quiet when you go in the house. *Gunsmoke* is about to start. Sit down and watch the show," Mother instructed her brood as we drove up to the farmhouse.

Mother and Daddy timed our arrival in plenty of time to settle their children before the television show started. If mother worked too late to arrive before 9:00 in the evening, we waited until Sunday morning. Nothing interrupted the Saturday night ritual.

We knew exactly what to expect. Granny and Granddaddy sat side-by-side in their matching recliners. My grandparents normally observed an early bedtime but not on

Saturday night. They owned a black and white console television but watched few shows. They preferred to spend free time singing or playing board games. Saturday evenings provided the exception. Whatever else happened on Saturday, the day ended with Marshall Dillon, Doc, and Miss Kitty.

The premier episode of *Gunsmoke* aired September 10, 1955 and remains the longest running prime-time television series of the twentieth century. For two decades James Arness and Milburn Stone portrayed Marshall Dillon and Doc Adams. Marshall Dillon kept the law in Dodge City, a wild-west town where people disrespected the law. Matt Dillon dealt with problems of frontier life. Cattle rustling, gunfights, and brawls required the Marshall's sound judgment and bravery. As the audience tuned in each week, they pieced together clues to the back-story of each character. The drama, though mild by modern standards, depicted a realistic view of the Western Frontier. *Gunsmoke* captured the courage, character, and spirit of the pioneers.

At the end of World War II, only a few thousand wealthy Americans owned a television. The average American relied on radios or newspapers for current events. Families gathered around the radio to listen to music, comedies, and dramas. A decade later televisions occupied a prominent position in two thirds of American homes. Though color televisions existed, most families purchased the more affordable black and white models. In 1954, the 15-inch black and white RCA model sold for less than $200, while the RCA color console cost approximately $1,000.

Every Saturday night at nine o'clock the music swelled, Marshall Dillon stepped into the street. The viewer watched as he slowly approached the villain, drew his gun, and fired. The announcer introduced the weekly episode "James Arness as Marshall Matt Dillon in *Gunsmoke*."

As a little girl, I disliked violence and hated the fight scenes. I hid my eyes until the conflict ended. I reasoned away the fear. *This isn't real. We don't live in the old west. Don't be scared.*

The familiar characters, Matt Dillon – Doc Adams – Miss Kitty – Chester – and later Festus – became as familiar as any real personality. My brother and cousins strapped on their toy gun belts and played *Gunsmoke*. The long dirt path between the house and the barn provided the perfect Main Street of our own personal Dodge City. The limited female role required me to serve drinks to the boys. Fortunately, we naively lacked understanding of the adult references. Every week provided a new story to embellish. When we tired of playing *Gunsmoke,* we switched to our own version of *Roy Rogers and Dale Evans* or The *Lone Ranger.*

Granddaddy rooted for Marshall Dillon to prevail over the outlaws. He identified with the hero's strong moral compass. The television western drew a clear line between good and evil. Good always triumphed by the end of each episode. Law and order prevailed and the world was safe for another week.

I Hate Snakes

When you see a rattlesnake poised to strike, you do not wait until he
has struck to crush him.
Franklin D. Roosevelt

I hate snakes – specifically rattlesnakes. My fear of snakes goes far beyond reasonable caution to near phobia. A simple photo of the slithering creatures sends shivers down my spine. My pulse quickens involuntarily at the mere thought of an actual encounter.

One early childhood experience led to my lifelong disdain of the venomous reptiles. Daddy and Uncle Buddy visited on the screened-in porch. They supervised my play as I chased Aunt Mary John's new puppy around the house. Suddenly, the dog stopped running. He barked furiously.

I stopped to see why the dog no longer circled the farmhouse. *What's wrong, you silly dog? Are you tired of our game?*

Suddenly, I felt Daddy sweep me into his arms and out of harm's way. In an unspoken plan, Daddy rescued me while my Uncle Buddy neutralized the threat.

They heard the dog's insistent barking and immediately saw the danger. The normally slow moving pair moved with uncharacteristic speed. The entire family poured out of the house and assured themselves of my safety. "One more step and she'd have stepped on the snake's head," the two men reported.

Their reaction frightened me more than the actual encounter. Playing outside at the farm changed that day. I no longer ran around recklessly. Instead, I anticipated danger and looked down more often than up. For the first time, I experienced fear.

Unfortunately, I lacked the maturity to distinguish between normal caution and irrational terror. I projected my fears onto even dissimilar reptiles.

Herpetologists identify more than ten rattlesnake species in Texas. The most common, western diamond-back, threatens Texans with aggressive behavior and venomous bites. The large body, triangular head, and characteristic rattle sets the species apart from other indigenous reptiles. Each time the snake molts, an interlocking scale attaches to the rattle. Muscular contractions create a rattling sound when the scales click together.

Rattlesnakes feed on rodents, reptiles, and insects. Their natural ambush hunting technique allows them to strike and inject unsuspecting prey with their venomous fangs. An adult rattler eats infrequently – needing food only once every two weeks. If threatened the snake may attack. Usually it takes a defensive position, shakes its rattle to warn predators, and can only strike from a coiled position. Normally, rattlesnakes avoid humans, and snakebites result when a person experiences the misfortune of crossing paths with the unfortunate creature.

"Good dog! Thanks for the warning," the family praised the puppy.

I cowered quietly in the corner. Sensing my continued anxiety, the little puppy uncharacteristically submitted to cuddling. The adults spoke in hushed whispers, unwilling for me to absorb their fears.

"So scary," I heard broken phrases from family members.

"Very lucky," uttered someone else.

"Thank God the dog warned us!" mother whispered prayerfully.

"Can we call the puppy, Lucky?" I chimed in.

Laughter interrupted the serious conversation and broke the tension. "That sounds like a really good name," Aunt Mary John agreed, "He's a lucky dog, and we are lucky to have him."

Horney Toad Passage to Alaska

Adventures do occur, but not punctually.
E.M. Forster, <u>A Passage to India</u>

In preparation for their Texas visit, the mom described strange creatures to her young son. Horned Lizards, known to us as horny toads, coexisted with many reptiles on the family farm. The West Texas area provided a perfect natural habitat for abundant lizard populations. Our distant cousins lived in Alaska and traveled to Texas for an extended visit.

The mother eagerly introduced her son to the differences between Texas and Alaska. We canvassed the farm, tramping through every usual sighting but found none of the normally plentiful species. Disappointed, they departed for home without locating a single horny toad.

TEXAS HORNED LIZARD *(Phrynosoma cornutum)*
SHORT-HORNED LIZARD *(Phrynosoma douglasi)*

The scientific name, Phrynosoma, means toad body. Commonly called horned frogs or horny toads because of their wide, flat bodies and the crown of horns on their heads, scales and claws cover the small reptiles. More than a dozen different species of horned lizards live throughout western North America. Two prominent horns at the rear and center of the skull distinguish the Texas Horny Toad from other species. Its unique coloring allows the lizard to blend into the landscape and hide from predators.

Texas horny toads feed primarily on harvester (red) ants. Harvester ants build large mounds with a hole in the center and remove the vegetation in a three to six foot circular pattern. Sightings of harvester ant mounds indicate the potential presence of horned lizards —both species like hot climates!

The horny toad's appearance and coloration provides an amazing defense by allowing it to blend into sparse vegetation. The creature's horns make it less palatable to predators. It can inflate itself to appear larger than its actual size. Its renowned ability to shoot a stream of blood from its eyelids frightens away predators, especially small children. Though horny toads prefer a diet of harvester ants, they also eat grasshoppers, beetles, and spiders quickly snapping them with a flick of the tongue and swallowing them whole.

Their foraging behavior puts them at risk from predators. Loss of habitat, use of pesticides, and overharvesting for pet trade led to a decrease in the population and resulted in protected status for the species. It currently requires a special permit to possess, transport, or sell horned lizards. Because horny toads demand specific conditions, they eventually die from improper care in captivity.

The Alaskan cousins barely arrived home, when the horny toads overran the farm. Mom decided we could create a habitat for the reptiles and send them to Alaska. Unfortunately, we didn't do our homework. We provided what we thought would sustain them for the trip. We poked holes in the box and added vegetation. We provided an inadequate diet – one without ants. We mailed the horny toads to the Alaska relatives. Not surprisingly, thanks to our inadequate research, the reptiles failed to survive the trip. (Note: We broke no laws. Legislation against transporting the Texas native reptile passed later in the century.)

Horned lizards share our Texas heritage. As children, we captured and played with horny toads. At the end of the day, we released them back to the dirt where they could survive, except for one attempted Alaskan adventure. We decreased the population by two. Never malicious – Definitely naïve – Valuable lesson learned – Don't mess with Texas Horny Toads.

A Legacy in a Little Square Cloth

Memory is a way of holding onto the things you love, the things you are, the things you never want to lose.
From the television show The Wonder Years

I remember this one. It was one of Granny's favorites. She kept it in her apron pocket.

As I unfolded, smoothed and refolded each square, I recalled the day I took possession of the vintage handkerchiefs. An impending move required sorting of Mother's treasures. She intended to choose a handkerchief for each of her granddaughters as a special Christmas gift from Grammer. We packed away Granny Carr's handkerchiefs, planning to present the girls with the special remembrance. Despite our best intentions, the handkerchiefs remained safely tucked away, all but forgotten.

Finally, I thought, *I'll carry out Mom's plan and present each of the girls with a special gift.*

Lovingly, I held each small cloth. I considered which design best matched the personality of each niece. Transported back in my memory to a time more than fifty years ago, I visualized Granny Carr to whom these handkerchiefs belonged. Each morning my grandmother retrieved one of the little square cloths from her dresser drawer and placed it in her apron pocket. It provided an essential accessory to her daily attire.

The history of handkerchiefs began in Ancient Rome where actors used white ones in comedies and satires. The Romans waved handkerchiefs at public games and dropping a hankie signaled the start of the chariot races. During the Middle Ages, a knight tied his lady's handkerchief to his helmet for good luck. Renaissance portraits depicted ladies holding finely embroidered handkerchiefs. Documents written by the courtiers described the use of a square piece of cloth to wipe the nose of Richard II of England, who ruled from 1377 to 1399. In Shakespeare's *Othello* a misunderstanding over a handkerchief caused Othello to kill his wife and then himself.

Initially a sign of wealth, royalty and status, the handkerchief became a part of every stylish European woman's wardrobe. Colonial women carried the tradition to America. Ladies in the nineteenth century added a personal touch to the normally white hanky by personally embroidering them with colorful flowers or images.

During the depression when a woman couldn't afford a new dress, she changed her wardrobe by changing her hankie at a price of five to fifty cents. Continuing through World War II, the handkerchief played a major role in fashion with colors and prints. Artists depicted images to decorate and celebrate events. Beyond the obvious use of wiping noses and drying tears, handkerchiefs served many purposes – from an easily accessible bandage to a triangulated pouch to hold a school lunch. Often a bride incorporated a handkerchief as a part of her bridal bouquet.

The birth of Kleenex sounded the death knell for handkerchiefs. Originally invented in the 1920s as a face towel to remove cold cream, by the 1930s advertisers touted Kleenex as the antidote to germs with their slogan "Don't carry a cold in your pocket."

While many women of the 1950s opted for the disposable Kleenex alternative, Granny Carr continued to use her handkerchiefs. She designated some for daily use, while she set aside special ones for Sunday dress. She tucked the brightly colored soft cloths into her apron pocket and pulled it out as necessary.

One particular afternoon Granny and I gathered plums from the garden. I reached for a plum at the exact moment a bee chose the same plum. Granny bandaged my finger in her hankie, took me to the house, removed the stinger, administered a paste of soda, rewrapped my finger in the hankie, and put my hand in a brown paper bag. The combination of a home remedy, the special hankie, and Granny's tender touch provided the exact healing my injured finger required.

Granny's hankies dried a river of tears, her own, as well as those of her children and grandchildren. Beyond physical tears, the soft squares soothed hurt feelings and wiped away emotional pain. Her gentle touch holding the handkerchief offered wordless comfort.

Some families inherit monetary wealth. The value of our family's inheritance outweighs anything money affords. The gift of the vintage handkerchief symbolizes intangible characteristics. Mary Verna Carr exhibited the strength required to survive difficult circumstances. She bequeathed her children with intangible characteristics of uncommon tenacity, resilience, and strength. A simple handkerchief preserved a reminder of this heritage and encouraged subsequent generations of young women to embrace their birthright.

Mother died October 2011, before she could present the handkerchiefs to her granddaughters. Christmas 2013, Verna Carr's great-granddaughters received one of her vintage handkerchiefs with a copy of this story.

The History of Aprons
Circulated via the Internet - Author Unknown

I don't think our kids know what an apron is.

The principal use of Grandma's apron was to protect the
dress underneath, because she only had a few, it was
easier to wash aprons than dresses and they used less
material but along with that, it served as a potholder for
removing hot pans from the oven.

It was wonderful for drying children's tears, and on
occasion was even used for cleaning out dirty ears.

From the chicken coop, the apron was used for carrying
eggs, fussy chicks, and sometimes half-hatched eggs to be
finished in the warming oven.

When company came, those aprons were an ideal hiding
places for shy kids.
And when the weather was cold grandma wrapped it
around her arms.

Those big old aprons wiped many a perspiring brow, bent
over the hot wood stove.
Chips and kindling wood were brought into the kitchen in
that apron.

From the garden, it carried all sorts of vegetables. After the peas had been shelled, it carried out the hulls.
In autumn, the apron was used to bring in apples that had fallen from the trees.

When unexpected company drove up the road, it was surprising how much furniture that old apron could dust in a matter of seconds.

When dinner was ready, Grandma walked out onto the porch, waved her apron, and the men folk knew it was time to come in from the paddocks to dinner.

It will be a long time before someone invents something that will replace that 'old-time apron' that served so many purposes.

Grandma used to set her hot baked apple pies on the windowsill to cool. Her granddaughters set theirs on the windowsill to thaw.

They would go crazy now trying to figure out how many germs were on that apron.

I never caught anything from an apron but love.

Granny's Apron

*"Women clad in aprons have traditionally prepared the
Thanksgiving meal, and it is within our historical linkage to share
our bounty."*
Ellyn Anne Geisel

Granny Carr always wore an apron. I rarely remember seeing her without one. It completed her everyday attire. Always stiffly starched and ironed, Granny's aprons included a bib and covered the entire front of her dress. Aprons served the purpose of a uniform. When she donned the apron, she prepared to work and taking it off signaled the end of the day's labor.

Many afternoons I sat at her feet, helping with the current day's task. Some days it might be shelling peas for the evening meal. The peas dropped into a mixing bowl, while the outer shells collected in the apron. Granny gathered the bottom corners of her apron, lifted the bundle, and carried the hulls to the trash. Similarly, the outer coverings of the pecan crop dropped into the apron, the pecan meat collected in a bowl, and Granny discarded the shells.

The afternoon schedule always allowed time for a nap or at least a break for resting quietly. Once awake from our nap, a paring knife emerged from the pocket of the apron to peel an apple or some other treat. The apron pocket often held surprise treats to delight her grandchildren.

I hated the hen house and dreaded the daunting task of gathering eggs. The hens really disliked being disturbed while "setting" on their eggs. Granny stuck her hand into the nest to shoo away the hens. I dodged as they flew directly at my face. No matter how much I anticipated the flight, they always startled and frightened me. Amazingly, I never remember Granny dropping or breaking an egg. She didn't own an egg basket. The apron gathered at the corners served as her egg carrier.

While some might consider a basket necessary to retrieve vegetables from the garden or fruit from the orchard, Granny chose to be unencumbered by containers. She gathered the corners of her apron and deposited fruits and vegetables in the pouch. In the case of a plentiful crop, she stepped into the kitchen, unloaded the produce into the sink, and returned to finish her harvest.

The pockets of the aprons sometimes served to hold bait or hooks on fishing trips to the riverbanks. On more than one occasion a fish or other reptile landed directly in Granny's apron covered lap.

The apron dried many children's tears and wiped many runny noses. Granny seemed unconcerned with spreading germs from a soiled apron. Despite the many tasks of the day, I never remember the apron looking dirty. If we ever gave it a thought, we never feared germs. Granny dropped her soiled apron in the laundry hamper and replaced it with a clean one. Granny worked hard without the advantage of most modern conveniences. An Iron? I own one today, but it is rarely if ever used. The electric iron represented a luxury. She ecstatically washed, starched, (in the days before spray starch) and ironed (without the benefit of a steam iron). She folded and placed the crisply pressed aprons in her dresser drawer. While she possessed little, she took good care of what she owned.

Granny's apron taught valuable life lessons. One item or tool served a multitude of uses. We own so much and could manage with much less. Remembering the fun we experienced on my Grandparent's farm makes me nostalgic for a simpler way of life. As I remember the challenges of my Granny's life, I am grateful for the wonderful conveniences that make my life so much easier. I am grateful for memories of Granny in her apron, instilling in me the value of hard work and good stewardship.

Like the unknown author of *The History of Aprons,* I never caught anything from Granny's apron but love.

Shelter from the Storm

"He who dwells in the shelter of the Most High will rest in the shadow of the Almighty. I will say of the Lord, "He is my refuge and my fortress, my God, in whom I trust."
Psalm 91:1 NIV

The storm cellar on my grandparent's farm terrified me. The closed cellar door provided a non-threatening place to explore and invent new games. The perfect height with just enough slant and a slick surface, the door served as a very wide slide for my siblings, cousins, and me.

Constructed to withstand the severe winds and tornadoes known to destroy entire farms, the cellar served as a safe harbor from frequent thunderstorms. Being unprotected from these storms risked serious injury and even death. My parents and grandparents witnessed enough damage to send them scurrying to the cellar when storm clouds gathered. Instead of depending on radio or television meteorologists to forecast the weather, they watched the skies and seemed to know instinctively which storms to weather in the farmhouse, and which ones necessitated a trip to the cellar.

Texas tornadoes, also called cyclones or twisters, historically occurred most often during April, May, or June. These storms often appeared suddenly and inflicted great damage in one brief blow. Strong Texas winds flattened entire towns, wiped out family farms, and claimed lives in minutes. April 1947, a tornado cut a trail 1½ miles wide and traveled a total of 221 miles across parts of Texas, Oklahoma, and Kansas. The funnel moved erratically across the ground, smashing some buildings, skipping others, and changing directions. In the aftermath of the storms oddities and freakish sights became Texas folklore – live plucked chickens, straws driven into posts, corn cobs imbedded in tree trunks, houses intact but shifted from foundations, whole large roofs displaced a few inches, and heavy equipment carried great distances. According to one account, a tornado in the Cedar Creek community in May 1868 "blew cattle into the air and lodged them in trees. It sucked all the water from the Brazos River for a short distance, and dumped a fifty-pound fish on dry land."

With the help of friends and neighbors, Granddaddy Carr excavated into a dirt embankment creating the family farm storm cellar, typical of most found in West Texas It opened into the ground, close enough to the house to provide easy access, yet far enough away to avoid dislodged material from trapping the family inside the cellar. The angle of the door allowed any debris or rubble from surrounding structures to slide off easily permitting the inhabitants to emerge.

Completely underground, with earthen walls, the dark, damp cellar served a dual purpose. Shelves lined the walls and provided a cool storage area for the canned vegetables from Granny Carr's garden. This proved especially

Typical West Texas Storm Cellar

helpful in days before the availability of refrigerators. The large underground room held enough provisions for weeks or even months. Often I ventured into the cellar with Granny to retrieve some of the canned provisions for the evening meal.

"That cloud looks bad. It's time to go to the cellar," Granddaddy announced.

No one questioned or hesitated. The women gathered the children and scurried out the back door and through the back yard. The unusual pace conveyed the urgency of the situation.

Like a cave, total darkness prevented any sight until the only source of light, a few oil lamps, illuminated the space. Musty odors offended the sense of smell. A single bed stood in the corner. The adults never slept during the storms. They disguised inward panic by calmly carrying out routine tasks. The women put the children to bed and tried to soothe us to sleep. *Really? Could sleep be possible?* Since I feared my grandfather's strict discipline, I closed my eyes and pretended to sleep as I listened to the adults discuss everything from the impending storm to events of the previous week and best of all, the latest gossip about friends and family members.

This secret little hideaway might sound like an exciting adventure for a curious little girl. However, the open cellar door revealed a terror of a different kind. The steep ten to twelve foot flight of stairs required some skill and balance. The underground vault, not entirely airtight, presented a very serious drawback. I often observed rattlesnakes killed and removed from that cellar. Granddaddy always entered the cellar first, checking for snakes and declaring the coast clear for the rest of us. Once the entire family gathered safely inside the cellar, Granddaddy ascended the stairs and closed the door. I trusted my grandfather completely, but always feared that perhaps one of the snakes might have escaped his watchful eye. My phobia of snakes far outweighed my fear of storms. I preferred to take my chances with the tornado rather than risk a remote chance of an encounter with a snake.

Personal experience justified my grandparent's fear of tornados. Momo Dooly suffered an almost irrational fear of storms. She remembered all too well May 6, 1930, the day of Texas tornadoes. For about twelve hours massive turbulence occurred from West Texas to deep East Texas and as far south as Kennedy in Karnes County. That morning windstorms struck Austin, Spur, and Abilene; from noon until 9:30 P.M., at least sixteen other places suffered severely. There were at least three separate tornadoes. Throughout the day, storms spread across the state, ravaging everything in its path. Eighty-two persons lost their lives because of the devastating storms. Damage totaled almost $2.5 million.

When Momo relocated to town with no storm cellar, she created her own shelter. Each time threatening clouds gathered, she confined my siblings and me under the dining room table as she anxiously paced and kept watch until the storm passed. We often added to her terror by making a game of escaping the shelter and playing chase through the house. Never one to follow rules and certainly not afraid of anything, my younger brother, George Michael, delighted in terrorizing our little grandmother. She spent many afternoons chasing him through the house in an effort to contain his little body but never his free spirit.

The many false alarms of my childhood created a reckless disregard for real storm danger. Often, like the "little boy who cried wolf" warnings that turn out to be "not so bad" caused a deaf ear to common sense precautions. Blissfully oblivious to the gathering storms, I often found myself caught in the middle of them, sometimes driving through torrential downpours making it impossible to see the road ahead or vehicles in my path.

Memories of the storm cellar and many afternoons spent under the dining table flooded my mind as I waited out the storms of May 15, 2013. The evening began with a normal routine. I navigated rush hour traffic through downtown to meet my daughter for our regular Wednesday dinner date. After dinner, Ginger headed to choir practice, and I made my way to the apartment. The dark clouds released a deluge. Safe inside, two thoughts occupied my mind. *Thank you, Lord, for safe travels through the storm* and *I hope Ginger stays at church until the storm passes.* With no satellite service, I prepared for a quiet evening with a good book.

An annoying racket signaling text messages shattered the silence. One after another, friends texted, *Are you in Dallas? Is Kerry okay? A tornado hit Granbury!* I phoned home. There had been a storm but my husband and everything at our house remained safely intact. Additional text messages assured the safety of family members in Granbury. The door opened and Ginger arrived safely. As I followed the reports of more tornados and storm damage, the warning sirens screamed. With minimal breaks, sirens continued for more than three hours. What started as a welcome rain for a dry land quickly escalated to a threatening storm. Like my anxious little grandmother, I watched the skies and prayed for all those affected by the storm.

As children, we mocked our little grandmother. Now, embarrassed by the way we tormented her, I understand the fear Momo felt and wish I could apologize for being so mean. Though still not terrified by storms, recent experiences developed respect for the power and fury of nature. The builder reinforced a closet in our home to serve as a safe room. Given access to the storm cellar, I'd be tempted to take refuge, but only if I could assure no snakes shared the space.

A Musical Inheritance

Music expresses that which cannot be put into words and that which cannot remain silent.

Victor Hugo

The old piano captured my pre-adolescent imagination. I dreamed of creating the kind of music I heard my mother and her sister produce from the keys. The treasured piece of furniture occupied a prominent place in the center room of Granny and Granddaddy Carr's farmhouse. Ornate carving and missing ivories supplied clues to the instrument's age. Its vintage turn of the century style seemed out of place at the center of the sparsely furnished parlor. If only the instrument could talk, what secrets might it reveal? Now I wonder – Then I never thought to ask. Had it been someone else's prized possession? Did it entertain audiences in a theater? Most likely, a newer model replaced it in the church, where the pianist accompanied congregational singing of hymns and gospel music. Whatever its origin, the tinny sounds provided my first exposure to the power of music.

Mrs. Cross lived on the hill about a mile from my grandparent's farm. She taught piano lessons. Neither of the Carr sisters showed much of an aptitude for reading music, or for learning shape notes. They disliked the discipline of practicing scales and playing music chosen by the teacher. Both displayed an uncanny talent for playing familiar songs, instinctively knowing which notes produced the melodies they heard. Soon they dropped out of lessons, preferring their own style of making music.

Music often brought the family together. Aunt Mary John positioned herself on the piano bench and signaled the family to gather. Though the tinny tone evidenced the instrument's better days, it still provided a sweet accompaniment for the voices that filled the evening hours. Granddaddy's booming speaking voice translated to a deep base singing voice. My daddy, George, sang base as well. When Granddaddy's brother visited, it added yet another deep bass voice to the ensemble. Mary John moved smoothly from one old hymn to another. Her strong soprano voice led the group. Mom's strong alto added rich harmonies. The entire family participated and nothing distracted from the music.

The text of old hymns provided my first theology lessons. I absorbed the messages by osmosis. Strains of *In the Sweet By and By* and *Shall We Gather at the River* reminded each of us of our eternal destination. *What a Friend We Have in Jesus* assured each one of Christ's presence.

I learned the power of music to bring people together. Whatever disagreements created discord earlier in the day melted away as music filled the room. The sweet spirit of family unity exceeded the musical harmony.

As much as I loved the family music gatherings, I loved the community sing even more. It offered a place to meet new people while honing performance skills. I learned about "open mike" performances long before anyone coined the phrase.

Sounds of music rang through the country air around the Trubey Community Center. The building, which historically served as the schoolhouse, now provided a gathering place for aspiring musicians. Any person brave enough – some talented and some less so – stepped on the stage and sang classic country and southern gospel.

I couldn't wait for the Saturday night gatherings. Young teens arrived with their families, but soon found our way outside to hang out unsupervised with our peers.

One Saturday evening the leader of my favorite group approached me. "Would you like to join our group? We need a girl singer."

My dry mouth prevented words from forming. The group included two of the cutest boys I knew. *Really? Could I? When do we practice?*

Terribly shy, I struggled to form relationships. Music expressed the deep emotions, my personality kept inside. I loved singing and I loved being a part of a group.

The whole family got into the act. Mother and her older sister sang with a variety of groups. Aunt Mary John presented my brother with a set of drums, and he quickly assimilated into the music community. My sister recalled her first public singing appearance, "Mother dressed us in matching dresses. We were probably four and six years old. Patty and I sang *Hey, Hey, Good Lookin'* to rave reviews."

The adorable little girls stole the show with a cuteness factor, which overshadowed their musically talented performance.

My love of music is rooted in those early days. My grandparents, my parents, and aunts taught me to love gospel music. The theology of the old songs continues to provide comfort for my soul. Often I recall the lyric of an old hymn exactly when I need encouragement.

The image of my family around the piano praising God evokes treasured memories. Each time I hear *In the Garden,* I visualize my Granddaddy standing at the end of that big upright, poorly tuned piano, singing his favorite hymn from his heart and soul.

Our family bestowed a love of music. We acquired an appreciation for all musical styles and passed it down to our children. The intrinsic worth of music enriches my life every day. It overcomes shyness - lifts spirits – gives joy – expresses emotions – provides a creative outlet – entertains – leads me into worship of my Lord. No other inheritance conveys anything more valuable. How could I ask for more?

Parents

"Parents can only give good advice or put them on the right paths, but the final forming of a person's character lies in their own hands."
Anne Frank

Finding Faith and Purpose

"Let every man abide in the calling wherein he is called and his work will be as sacred as the work of the ministry. It is not what a man does that determines whether his work is sacred or secular; it is why he does it."

A.W. Tozer, The Pursuit of God

Two idealistic cousins fidgeted on the front pew of Noodle Baptist Church. Neither possessed the life experience to anticipate the life challenges ahead. Though the combined ceremony conferred the title of minister on both young men simultaneously, each clearly understood the individual nature of the covenant tonight's service confirmed. The public ritual commemorated a private commitment to God's plan.

James and Wallace shared much more than the common ordination date. They grew up playing and working together on the family farms. First cousins, they shared the bond of a close-knit community and even closer-knit family. They fished and hunted together. They attended the same church and heard the same sermons.

The congregation prepared to ordain Bettie Williams' grandsons. The leaders of the rural Baptist church knew the young men and their families well. They watched the boys develop characteristics essential to the ministry. A council of ministers and deacons examined the candidates and voted to proceed with the ordination.

Pastor V. D. Walters mentored the aspiring ministers as they planned the special worship experience. Each young man prepared to share his conversion experience as well as his call to the ministry. They invited spiritual mentors to participate in the service and planned every detail. The date finally arrived. They waited nervously for the service to begin.

Conversations quieted as Jack Benningfield, a respected community leader known for his deep bass voice, stepped behind the pulpit. James' sister, Theda Bell Williams, took her place at the piano. Jack led the congregation in singing songs of commitment chosen by the candidates. They sang hymns of commitment and surrender including *Wherever He Leads I'll Go* and *I Surrender All*.

Juanita, Wallace's bride of less than a month, grew up singing in the Amity Church. Hiding her anxiety well, she proudly took her place at the pulpit and sang. Although no one preserved a program for the service, I imagine her singing a favorite hymn *I'd Rather Have Jesus*.

Dictated by tradition, the pastor of the church provided a "charge to the candidates." Pastor V. D. Walters spoke directly to the young men and charged them to remain true to their calling. He directed them to set examples as men of good character. He spoke about the challenges ahead. First James and then Wallace spoke to the audience filled with family, friends, and neighbors who remembered them as infants, little boys, and now as young men. Each shared a unique salvation experience and spoke of his desire to follow God's plan for his life. Brother Walters delivered an ordination message urging individual parishioners to follow God. The service concluded with a "charge to the church" given by a deacon. Possibly, Wallace's new father-in-law, John Carr, admonished the church to support, encourage, and pray for the newly commissioned ministers.

As Wallace's bride listened to her husband and his cousin describe their personal relationship with Jesus, she doubted. *I know I've been baptized, but I don't have the assurance and the personal relationship they describe.*

Years later, Wanda Juanita, would share her own spiritual journey with her children. "I was the daughter of a Baptist deacon. We were at church every time the door opened. As a young girl, I walked down the aisle, joined the church, and was baptized. As a young wife, I doubted my relationship with God. Every time I went to church, I felt an uncomfortable nudging. I needed to be sure of my salvation. I asked Christ into my heart. It was hard to make the decision public. I was embarrassed but knew this was an important step. I went to the front of the church and shared my choice."

When the weather warmed, her husband baptized her in the Clear Fork of the Brazos River.

James Williams served as a bi-vocational pastor of Southern Baptist Churches throughout West Texas. He worked at a number of jobs, including one as a school janitor at the Noodle School, to support his wife and children.

By his twenty-first birthday, George Wallace Dooly welcomed the first of four children. He enrolled in classes at Hardin Simmons University. He performed weddings, funerals, and preached when he got the opportunity. Unfortunately, his wife discouraged him, pointing out his shortcomings in sermon delivery. Discouraged and struggling financially, he dropped out of school and pursued a career as a plumber.

When their twenty-year marriage ended in divorce, George questioned whether he misunderstood God's voice. *Well, if God intended me to serve as a pastor, that's over now. God forgives any sin, including divorce. However, no church allows a divorced pastor.*

His moral values and his Christian commitment remained strong. Though he'd given up the dream of ministry, he continued to sense God's call. *Maybe I'm supposed to serve God in my daily work life.*

I spent an afternoon with my dad shortly before his death. "What was your favorite thing about your job?" I asked.

"I really liked helping the young plumbers figure out the solution to problems they couldn't resolve. I especially enjoyed taking calls from the public and saving them money by telling them how to fix their problem themselves without a service call. When they needed a plumber, we had a customer for life. It was about doing the right thing."

George and his second wife, Helen, joined a non-denominational church near their home. When their pastor moved away, the congregation invited George to preach. The temporary situation evolved to a new career. For almost two decades, he served as the pastor of the small church. He connected with the ministerial alliance and served as an active volunteer for the Salvation Army.

The last season of Daddy's life proved the most fulfilling. The years spent in a secular job produced trust and endurance. He wasted no part of his life. Hard work, financial struggles, a failed marriage, grief, and loss prepared him to serve his congregation. He understood them, because he walked in their shoes.

George W. Dooly

February 26, 1950, two young men stood before a small West Texas congregation and promised to serve God with their lives. Both fulfilled their vows. My father modeled the importance of integrity and of viewing work through the lens of service - whether the service is in the secular workplace or within the walls of a church.

Whatever you do, work at it with all your heart, as working for the Lord, not for human masters, since you know that you will receive an inheritance from the Lord as a reward. It is the Lord Christ you are serving.
Colossians 3:23-24 NIV

General Guidelines for Ordination and License for Ministry

Note: This information is included to explain the significance place on license and ordination of ministers.

http://media.mobaptist.org/public/pastoral-ministry/GeneralGuidelinesforOrdinationandLicense.pdf

Every Southern Baptist church is autonomous and establishes its own policies. However, there are some traditional practices, which seem to be followed by most of our churches. Each local church determines whom they will ordain. Associations, state conventions, or the Southern Baptist Convention do not ordain.

License:

The licensing is the church's tentative approval for a man to serve until he has proved himself qualified for ordination. In regard to the practice of granting a license for a minister, the following steps are usually taken:

1. The person to be licensed makes a public decision in the church and expresses his feeling that God is specifically calling him to ministry.

2. He requests the church to grant him a license.

3. The church votes on the request to grant the license.

4. A "Certificate of License" (which can be purchased at a Christian bookstore) is filled out and presented to the minister.

Ordination

Ordination usually takes place when a minister begins serving in a church. In regard to

Ordination the following are the traditional steps:

1. A church calls a minister as pastor or to a position in some field of ministry (such as education, music, youth, etc.).

2. The church who calls the person may perform the ordination, or request the minister's home church to perform the ordination.

3. The pastor, a minister, or the chairman of deacons of the ordaining church presents the request to the church and asks for permission to convene an Examining Council or an Ordination Council. The church should not be hasty in ordaining an individual. It should be certain he has the scriptural qualifications to serve as a minister. The candidate should prove himself before he is considered for ordination.

4. If the request is approved, a time and place is established for the Ordination Council and ordained persons (deacons and ministers) are invited. These may be persons who are members of that particular church as well as ordained persons from other churches. Either a formal invitation or a letter of invitation should be sent to the neighboring Baptist Churches inviting all ordained persons to participate in the ordination council. If the questioning of the candidate and the ordination

service is to be conducted on the same day the invitation can include inviting all interested persons to the ordination service.

5. The pastor, a minister, the director of missions, or the chairman of deacons presides over the Ordination Council until a chairman is elected. The chairman leads in the questioning of the person to be ordained. Usually the person being ordained is seated so that he is facing those who are asking questions. Any person who is present may ask questions. Usually the person being ordained is asked to briefly tell of his conversion experience and also his call to the Gospel Ministry. Other questions may be centered around Biblical theology, ethics, morals, personal beliefs, etc.

6. The Ordination Council votes on whether to recommend that the church proceed with the ordination of the candidate. The council may choose to delay the ordination or even reject the candidate. That is why it may be best to hold the council one week prior to the ordination service.

7. If the Council votes to recommend ordination, the pastor or chairman of the Ordination Council presents the recommendation to the church, either at a regular business meeting or a called business meeting, for church approval.

8.If the church approves, a date for an Ordination service is set. The service follows the order of a regular worship service with modifications. Someone (or two people) may give

a "charge to the candidate" and a"charge to the church" Appropriate music is selected. Someone may preach an ordination sermon. Someone will pray an ordination prayer and ordained persons will "lay on hands." The person being ordained may be presented a

Bible and along with his wife and family receive the congratulations of the people after the benediction. The service should be not more than one hour in length.

9. A Certificate of Ordination is presented (may be purchased at a Christian book store or printed on a good computer). Most churches in the area combine the ordination council and the ordination service into one. The disadvantage of this method is that there could be great embarrassment for the candidate and to the church if the ordination council voted not to recommend ordination.

The Final Gift

"People are like stained-glass windows.
They sparkle and shine when the sun is out, but when the darkness
sets in; their true beauty is revealed only if there light is from
within."
Elizabeth Kubler Ross

"I'm going to Elliot's. Do you want to go with me?"
Mom's tone indicated more of a demand than an invitation.

I never declined Mom's request to accompany her on
these late evening missions. I sensed she needed, more than
wanted me to go along. An attendant answered the bell,
unlocked the front door, and escorted Mother to one of the
back rooms. The front parlor of Elliott's Funeral Home
provided a calm, quiet place with few distractions. The late
hour assured only the staff and the deceased occupied the
building. All visitors departed long before Mom and I
arrived.

I unpacked my notebook and proceeded to busy
myself with homework. I spent many evenings at Elliott's
immersed in my textbooks. If I finished my schoolwork, a
good book diverted my attention from the purpose of our
visit and the work occurring in the back room.

Prior to the Civil War, most families cared for their
own dead. In some rural areas of the United States, families
continued to perform the necessary preparation and burial
rituals until after the turn of the century. As embalming
became an accepted practice, the family-owned funeral

home emerged as a necessary service to the local community.

Three generations of the Elliott-Hamil family served the bereavement needs of Abilene for decades. Pete and Mittie Elliott founded Elliott's Funeral Home in 1933. Their daughter, Jo Ann and her husband John Hamil, joined them in the business in 1950s. The Hamil's son, Robert, followed them in the family business. During the sixties, they enlisted my mother to provide a necessary service.

After the embalming procedure, the staff prepared the body for viewing. The process included dressing, applying cosmetics, and styling the deceased's hair. Not knowing the individual provided a necessary emotional detachment. However, anonymity also presented a challenge. How can you make someone appear natural when you have no idea how they wore their hair and makeup? Photos helped but failed to substitute for knowing the individual's personal taste and style.

Mother's customers visited her salon regularly. She curled and styled their hair weekly. She knew exactly what each lady liked and more importantly, what she disliked. She understood the importance of hands and nails. She listened as the women shared their hopes, dreams, and disappointments. She valued her patrons and considered them friends. She watched them age and decline. When they could no longer come to the salon, she visited them and continued to provide services in their homes whenever possible.

Her connection with Elliott's began when the family of one of her beloved customers asked her to come to the funeral home and style their mother's hair. After all, who knew better how she liked it? Mother reluctantly agreed. She anticipated the emotional cost of such an experience. She often attended funerals but never touched a lifeless body.

She procrastinated as long as possible before driving the short distance to the funeral parlor. The bright white exterior of the building stood in stark contrast to her dark mood. *Lord, help me do this.* She breathed a silent prayer as she opened the car door and forced her feet to plod toward the entrance.

"I'll be right here with you and help you with anything you need," the funeral director assured her.

Drops of salty liquid rolled down her cheeks as she gazed into the familiar but lifeless face of her old friend. She recalled the last of their many conversations and wished for one final opportunity to express her friendship.

"Are you ready to start?" a voice brought her back to reality and the purpose of her visit.

"As ready as I'll ever be," she responded.

She spent hours working diligently to achieve a perfect result before she finally announced, "It's as perfect as I can make it."

Exhausted, she washed her hands, discarded the used apron, and left the building. Alone in her car, she wept. The difficult task proved rewarding and offered a surprising sense of accomplishment. She recognized the importance of this special gift and knew she would return. However, she determined never to come alone. On every subsequent visit, one of her daughters accompanied her.

As a preschooler, I attended the funerals of my grandfather and my great-grandmother. For months following the services, I experienced nightmares of the caskets and dead bodies. Not surprisingly, I lacked curiosity or desire to understand the logistics of Mother's task. I contentedly waited for her in the serene lobby.

We chatted about ordinary subjects on the drive to the funeral home and rarely talked on the way home. I wondered at her peaceful demeanor. One evening I broached the subject. "Isn't it a little creepy, touching a corpse? How do you do it?"

"At first it was strange. However, I decided to change the way I looked at things. Now, instead of focusing on the lifeless body, I remember something special about the person and her influence on my life. I think of this as the last service I can provide for my friend."

With that brief answer, I learned much about my mother. She worked long, hard hours. She never volunteered time or money to causes. She chose one volunteer opportunity. She used her unique talents to provide a necessary service as a final gift.

Everyone experiences death, loss, and grief. Rituals allow families and friends to express sadness, say goodbye and celebrate the life of someone they loved. By her example, Mother taught her children the importance of an act of kindness. She conveyed the importance of being present for a hurting friend and communicated the intrinsic rewards of doing the right thing.

Elliott-Hamil Funeral Home

Memories of Growing up

"Someday you will be old enough to start reading fairy tales again."
C.S. Lewis

Daddy's Little Princess
Meeting Dorothy and the Wonderful Wizard of Oz

"Old theatres are irreplaceable. They could never be duplicated at today's costs – but more importantly, their spirit could not be duplicated because they remind us of a day when going to the show was a more glorious and escapist experience. I think a town's old theatres are the sanctuary of its dreams."
Roger Ebert

"Where are we going?" I eagerly inquired as Daddy helped me onto the front seat of the family car, a position normally reserved for my mother.

Instinctively I sensed something different about this outing. Dressed in our Sunday best, we set out on a rare father-daughter outing. "It's a surprise. You'll see when we get there."

For four years, I enjoyed being the center of my parent's world. Everything changed with the arrival of my baby brother ten days before my fourth birthday. He demanded constant attention, leaving me to entertain myself.

The 1955 re-release of the *Wizard of Oz* gave Daddy the perfect opportunity to shower his undivided attention on me. He introduced me to Dorothy, the Wizard, and all the colorful characters of Oz long before I could read the mystical story.

I treasured books, carefully turning each page. When none of the grown-ups read to me, I created my own stories

211

from the pictures. The printed stories of *Oz* required much more focus than my four-year-old attention span allowed. However, in contrast to reading, the movie with its constant stimulation and engaging music promised to mesmerize any child. I imagined myself a princess as we found our seats inside Abilene, Texas' historic downtown theater for the first time. Everything about the venue supported my princess fantasy.

Built by H. O. Wooten, The Paramount Theater opened in 1930. The interior boasted a Spanish-Moorish architectural theme. Grand archways beckoned visitors into the auditorium or up the stairway to the balcony.

Heightened senses took in every detail of the theater's grandeur.

The aroma

Paramount Theater - Summer 2016

of hot, buttered popcorn beckoned customers downstairs to the concession counter. Only the strongest appetite resisted the temptation to taste the warm treat. The opulent Hollywood-style lounge allowed young girls to live out movie star fantasies. Gold-framed mirrors reflected the image of the individual patron. *Yes, indeed, I do look fine.*

Cushioned, comfortable seats encouraged guests to linger and escape reality if only for a couple of hours. Passing clouds and twinkling lights adorned the domed ceilings creating the visual sensation of a starry sky. A heavy red curtain concealed the screen, adding to the mystery of the story soon to be revealed.

Finally, the curtain lifted, and music called the audience to attention. The feature began, and I moved to the edge of my seat, sitting up as tall as possible. Wide-eyed, I eagerly focused on the screen. I watched with rapt attention as the tornado swept Dorothy and Toto from Kansas, down the yellow brick road to the Land of Oz.

For years, I imagined myself as Dorothy dancing in ruby red slippers, down the yellow brick road and singing about a visit to *The Wizard*. I identified with her desire to escape reality and the challenges of life. Like Dorothy, I wondered if bluebirds fly over the rainbow, why I

Interior of the Paramount

couldn't do the same. The yearly television screening of the movie kept the story fresh and alive in my memory.

My first movie experience left a permanent impression. It opened Hollywood's fantasy world. Movies and music provided a life-long, healthy coping mechanism.

During my teen years, date nights sometimes afforded the opportunity to experience the Paramount from a different perspective. One memorable evening, we saw Audrey Hepburn in *Wait Until Dark*. For weeks, I replayed the thriller in my head. Each night, I'd turn off the light, half expecting the intruder to grab my foot as I darted across the room.

Though modern movie theaters fail to equal the Paramount experience, I still love the movies. Movie nights at home offer a comfortable alternative, but nothing beats hot, buttered popcorn and a good movie on the big screen.

Fully restored in 1986, the historic Paramount Theater opens for daily tours and continues to present classic films and live performances. Sitting quietly in the empty theater, I recall my first visit. For a moment, I return to childhood. Once again I am Daddy's little princess, if only for one marvelous afternoon.

The Gift of Life

"There are two ways to live: you can live as if nothing is a miracle; you can live as if everything is a miracle."
Albert Einstein

"Wake up," Daddy shook me gently.

The partially closed bathroom door allowed just enough light for me to focus on my Daddy's face. "What time is it? It's Saturday. We don't have school. I don't have to get up." I mumbled groggily.

"It's 4:00 a.m. The baby's coming. I'm taking your mother to the hospital. Please take care of your brother and sister until I get back home. You're a big girl. I know you can handle this."

Though my grandmother lived with us, my parents expected me to care for the children. My maturity surpassed my almost ten years, and I took the responsibility quite seriously.

In the days before sonograms, no one knew the sex of a baby before the birth. My six-year-old brother and I redefined sibling rivalry. We fought over everything. I doted on my two-year old sister and prayed for a sister rather than another brother.

The phone rang an hour later. "We barely made it to the hospital before the baby came. You have another sister."

I ran through the house, squealing excitedly. "It's a girl! Her name is Lisa. Yahoo! We have another sister!"

Each of us played a distinct role in our relation with Mom. Still in her teens when I arrived, Mother practiced her parenting skills on me. She often treated me as an equal. She confided in me, her first- borne child, in the same way she spoke to a friend. None of us questioned Lisa's status as the baby and Mother's favorite. We all knew it and never questioned why. One poignant conversation provided an explanation for her favoritism. Mom waited until I understood the complexities of conception, before she detailed the circumstances of Lisa's birth.

She reported a history of gynecological health problems and a scheduled D&C. The physician planned the surgery, and Mother arranged her work schedule months ahead. Her menstrual cycle irregularities failed to indicate pregnancy. Though no one else suspected, she knew her own body.

The family struggled financially, and an unplanned pregnancy complicated the already troubled marriage. *I could go through with the procedure. It's early. A pregnancy test will be negative. No one will know. But, God knows and I know. I could never live with myself.*

"I'm pregnant," she informed the physician when she called to cancel the procedure.

Mother recognized the life within her as a special blessing. Through the years, she often referred to Lisa as God's special gift to her.

Lisa learned the circumstances of her birth as an adult when I shared this story with her after Mother died. Imagine my surprise. I assumed she knew. It never occurred to me

Mother would withhold such an important piece of history from her favorite child.

Neither Mother nor Daddy ever indicated an understanding of the meaning of our names. Instead, they chose our names based on family connections or simply names they liked. My mother first heard Lisa's name on a soap opera. Her middle name honored our pastor, Arlie Watson.

Though Mother and Daddy failed to appreciate the meaning of names, Lisa attaches a great deal of importance to her name. She embraces and lives in its significance. Lisa means God's promise. An Irish origin, the name Arlene means an oath, or pledge. Knowing the details of her conception and birth confirmed Lisa's commitment to fulfill her calling - God's promise.

Complicated family bonds defy explanation. I share history with my siblings. They understand my quirky little habits without explanation or back-story. They get it. We count on each other for love and support in the good, the bad, and the ugly times of life.

Roe versus Wade legalized abortion thirteen years after my baby sister arrived. My mother could have ended the pregnancy, and no one would have been the wiser. What a tragedy that would have been! The world is a better place because my mother chose life!

The World's Largest Concrete Swimming Pool

"At the end of your life, you will never regret not having passed one more test, not winning one more verdict, or not closing one more deal. You will regret time not spent with a husband, a friend, a child, a parent."
Barbara Bush

Mother never learned to swim. To my knowledge, she didn't own a bathing suit. Swimming pools and lakes terrified her. Her bucket list never included dipping her toes in the ocean. I once teasingly asked, "Do you need a life jacket to take a bath?"

Consequently, the joy of teaching his children to swim fell to Daddy. Unlike my mother, he really enjoyed the water. He loved going to the river. Most often, he fished from the bank of the Clear Fork of the Brazos. Sometimes, he escaped the heat by wading into the creek for a quick swim.

"Please let me go swim," Patty begged.

"No! You're just getting over strep throat. I don't want you to get sick again," Mother emphatically commanded.

The conversation ended – no amount of arguing could change her mind. The family worked together unpacking the picnic lunch and spreading the blanket where mother sat with her middle daughter. Daddy headed to the gigantic pool with Patty's three siblings. Granny and Granddaddy entertained the disappointed little girl.

I sympathized with my little sister but not enough to miss the opportunity to plunge into the pool. Daddy carried my baby sister, while my brother ran ahead of us. I surveyed the pool, trying to decide which area I wanted to explore first.

The adventure began early in the morning. Mom fried chicken and packed enough food to feed a small army. All four children climbed into the back seat of the car to ride for an hour east to Cisco, Texas. We anticipated seeing aunts and uncles and our grandparents. However, the Cisco Swimming Pool exceeded expectations. Our parents surprised us with the destination, billed as the largest swimming pool in the world, and all it offered.

In the early 1920s, an inadequate water supply plagued Cisco. The citizens of the small town built Williamson Dam, resulting in Lake Cisco and creating the largest concrete swimming pool in the world. For decades, the pool provided a major attraction for the Central West Texas area. Celebrities like Bob Wills entertained at the bandstand. Hundreds of people watched from the steps as beauties paraded across the bridge and island while competing in local pageants.

Fresh, non-chlorinated, water from the spillway fed the swimming pool, allowing live fish to swim by the legs of human visitors. An island divided the shallow end of two to four feet from the twenty-five foot deep end. A massive slide rose from the island and landed in the shallow end.

Swing sets invited children and their parents to drop from the swings into the pool. The deep end's most obvious attraction featured a forty-four foot tall diving tower with four levels 11 feet apart, though few divers dared to leap from the top deck.

Other attractions included a two-story skating rink, a miniature golf course, picnic grounds, an amusement park, and the remnants of an abandoned zoo. At one time, the hollow dam allowed public visitors. The blackness of the inner chamber provided a spookier atmosphere than any horror movie.

When baby girl Lisa tired, Daddy returned her to the blanket to rest with Mother and Patty. He returned to the water and played with Mike and me. "Please, can we slide?" we begged.

It took very little convincing. We swam to the island, and he eagerly joined us as we climbed to the top. Once at the top, I trembled with fear. "Don't look down," Daddy encouraged. "I'll go first and be at the bottom to catch you."

Though I could barely see him at the bottom of the slide, I trusted him to catch me. I turned loose and flew down the slide to the cool water below. When Daddy caught me, I wasn't eager to repeat the slide. I suggested the next adventure, "That was fun. Now, let's go try out the swing,"

After our picnic, we crawled back into the car. Worn out but contented from a day in the world's largest swimming pool, two of the Dooly kids happily rested on the way home. The youngest barely remembers being there and the other only remembers the disappointment of not being able to swim with the rest of us.

We didn't realize we were making memories,
We just knew we were having fun.
Unknown

Christmas Eve Memories

"When we recall Christmas past,
we usually find that the simplest things – not the great occasions –
give off the greatest glow of happiness."
Bob Hope, American film actor and comedian.

Daddy sat in the driver's seat, allowing the car (and heater) to run. Three granddaughters surrounded our little grandmother. No one seemed to mind being crammed in the back seat of the blue and white, ten-year-old Buick sedan. Mike took his place in the front seat separated from his sisters to avoid inevitable bickering. Leaving Momo in charge of the children, Daddy returned to the house to see what detained Mom.

"What's taking so long?" the brood whined to no one in particular.

After what seemed like an eternity to the excited children, Mom and Dad emerged from the house. *Finally, we're on the way!*

First stop – a visit to Santa at the Mrs. Baird's Bakery. Eager children stood in a long line for a turn to share their Christmas list with Santa. Some waited patiently, certain Santa watched to see if they behaved. Others fidgeted, unable to contain their excitement. Some parents waited in line with their children. My parents entrusted my sisters and brother to my watchful eyes, while they waited on the ground below. We patiently climbed the steep stairway to the top, where the elves helped us climb into Santa's sleigh.

Microphones and large speakers enabled the crowd to hear each child's Christmas list. Parents below panicked when the child added another item – a total surprise – no way the gift would be waiting on Christmas morning. They scrambled to explain Santa's inability to fulfill every wish. Finally, our turn to talk to Santa – mission accomplished – Santa knew exactly what we wanted under the tree.

While I waited in line with my siblings, the aroma of freshly baked bread filled the air and made my mouth water. The warmth of the ovens welcomed us inside from the cold. Touring the bakery completed the traditional visit. The employees explained the process of making, packaging, and delivering bread. Knowing a mini loaf of bread waited at the end of the line made it difficult for me to listen. Finally, I received a slice of hot buttered bread. The first bite of the delicious treat melted in my mouth, fulfilling every expectation.

Next stop – Thornton's Department Store windows entertained visitors long after the store closed for the day's business. Throughout the 1950s, animated figures created Christmas magic for the children of Abilene. Characters brought scenes to life. One window featured Snow White and the dwarves, while bears danced in another window. Each year the windows remained covered until the unveiling ceremony. Families parked cars and strolled on the sidewalk to get a closer look at minute details. Children imagined themselves a part of the scene. Parents huddled near their children and experienced the wonder of the season through their children's eyes. Other more scientific minds stood amazed at the technical expertise and pondered what made the animation work. Most visitors simply enjoyed the beauty and artistry.

"Look at that one," Mother pointed excitedly at an especially pretty costume or a captivating scene. She lost herself in the magic of the animation, and enjoyed the windows as much as any child.

The adventure continued as we piled back into the car and set off to look at Christmas lights in the neighborhoods around town. Christmas Eve presented a rare occasion – a night both Mom and Dad took a break from their usual work schedule. The nuclear family came together – no arguments – no bickering – we simply enjoyed the tastes, sights, and sounds of Christmas.

After a full evening, we returned home to the best surprise of all. While we visited Santa at Mrs. Baird's, Thornton's windows, and looked at the pretty Christmas lights, Santa visited our house, leaving lots of presents underneath the Christmas tree. We never questioned Santa's ability to be in two places at the same time. The four of us eagerly tore into the gifts selected especially for us.

Only a few specific gifts stand out in my memory. I always loved music, even as a little girl. One year I begged for a record player. Mother prepared me, "A record player is really expensive. Santa might not be able to afford such an extravagant gift. Besides, I bet Santa might think you're too young and not responsible enough to deserve such a special thing."

I prepared myself for inevitable disappointment. Mom convinced me Santa couldn't possibly bring something so special to me. She watched my face to experience the surprise and excitement when I received exactly what I wanted. I wore out the only records I owned, playing them over and over and over again. I bet my parents sickened of Elvis Presley's *Teddy Bear* and *Hound Dog* before I earned enough allowance to add another record to the collection.

Another memorable Christmas, I received my first bicycle. I waited until Christmas afternoon for the bike-riding lesson. Daddy ran along beside me. I fell several times before I accomplished the balance to go ride alone. Confident in my ability, he let go and watched as I promptly crashed head on into a big tree on the edge of the sidewalk. The collision left a permanent dent in my shiny new bike. I eventually learned to ride my bike, but not on Christmas Day.

One gift left a lasting impression for an entirely different reason. I started driving at sixteen. I took the responsibility seriously, but the lack of training and experience made me a poor driver. December 1967, I took the car to Burrow Alley for a Christmas shopping excursion. The newly developed area provided some unique gift ideas. I don't remember what I bought that day. However, I vividly remember the event that ruined the year's Christmas season for me. In a moment of poor judgment, I pulled forward rather than backing out of the parking place, not noticing the short curb between my tires. The momentary lapse resulted in the loss of the car's muffler.

Neither of my parents said much about the incident. My dad replaced the muffler. I felt relieved at the lack of consequences. On Christmas Eve as we opened gifts, the largest package under the tree belonged to me. I opened the heavy box to find the old rusty broken muffler. Mom laughed hysterically. Though I received an appropriate gift, I remember only the gag gift. I failed to be amused. Obviously, Mother and I differed in our interpretation of humor.

Each Christmas Eve ended when Mom and Dad quieted their excited children. Dressed in our pajamas, we gathered around them. Dad opened his Bible and read the Christmas story. We went to bed with the words of Luke and the true meaning of Christmas fresh in our minds.

Christmas Day celebrations focused on food and family. Granny, Mom and her sisters spent hours preparing decadent desserts and traditional holiday treats. We gathered each year at my grandparents' farmhouse for time with the extended family.

Even as a young child, I understood the importance of making Christ the center of Christmas. My parents bestowed an intangible gift. They taught us to focus on Jesus and serve others.

My best Christmas memories focus not on the gifts, under the tree. Instead, I remember the traditions and the love we shared. When we celebrate the true meaning of the season, gifts pale in comparison.

In the same region, shepherds were staying out in the fields and keeping watch at night over their flock.

There an angel of the Lord stood before them, the glory of the Lord shone round them, and they were terrified.

But, the angel said to them.

"Don't be afraid, for look. I proclaim to you good news of great joy that will be for all the people. Today a Savior who is Messiah, the Lord, was born for you in the city of David.

This will be the sign for you. You will find a baby wrapped snugly in cloth and lying in a feeding troth.

Suddenly, there was a multitude of heavenly host with the angel, praising God and saying:

"Glory to God in the highest heaven and peace on earth to people whom He favors!"

Luke 2: 8-14 NIV

Scoggins Downtown Beauty Corral

"It is my considered opinion that the hairdresser is the most influential person in any community. When the public goes to a hairdresser, something happens to them. They feel safe, they relax. The hairdresser knows what their skin is like under the makeup; they know their age; they don't have to keep up any kind of pretense. People tell a hairdresser things they wouldn't dare confess to a priest and they are open about matters they try to conceal from a doctor. When people place their secret lives in the hairdresser's hands, the hairdresser gains an authority few other people attain. I have heard hairdressers quoted with complete conviction on art, literature, politics, economics, childcare, and morals. I tell you that a clever, thoughtful, ambitious hairdresser wields a power beyond the comprehension of most people."
John Steinbeck

The unique salon boasted a western motif and contrasted sharply with the opulent Windsor Hotel lobby. Lavish furnishings welcomed guests to the hotel. Bellhops and elevator attendants catered to the visitor's every need. Luxurious surroundings promised a deluxe experience.

A western clad cowgirl receptionist greeted guests who entered the salon from the hotel lobby. A large L-shaped wooden bar served as the focal point of the reception area. A boot-rail added to the authentic feel of stepping up to a western saloon bar. Ranch brands added to the cowboy experience. Past the reception desk, individual stations provided a distinctive experience. No element detracted from the old west atmosphere.

The owner's magnetic personality filled the salon and attracted patrons including celebrity clientele. Pictures of George Scoggins and his famous clients hung in the lobby of the Scoggins Beauty Corral.

One especially fascinating character frequented the salon on his professional visits to Abilene. In the early 1950's, George Wagoner, AKA Gorgeous George, relied on hairstylists to support his flamboyant stage personality. George perfected a role as an arrogant, platinum blonde villain and entertained wrestling enthusiasts. The wrestler entered the ring to "Pomp and Circumstance" wearing robes of lace and fur. George enraged the audience just by walking into an arena. He became the villain wrestling fans loved to hate. His flamboyant personality played well to new television audiences. His reputation for cheating and fighting dirty enhanced the pre-show exploits. When officials attempted to check his robes for foreign objects, he gained fame by shouting at the officials, "Get your filthy hands off me."

His hairstyle provided a key element to the wrestler's signature persona. He entered the arena with perfectly coiffed, platinum blonde curls. Before each match, he dramatically removed *Golden Georgie Pins* and tossed them to ladies in the audience. His hairstyle required perfection to support the image. Mr. Scoggins proudly displayed a picture with Gorgeous George sporting a Scoggins styled masterpiece.

Professional wrestling dominated one of the two available television channels each Saturday night. I hated the violence. Any activity provided a better alternative to observing the flamboyant costumes and phony theatrics. Despite my personal distaste for the sport, I understood the importance of the picture in Mr. Scoggins' gallery.

I loved visiting the salon and viewing the collection of photos. My fascination with the photo of Gorgeous George paled in comparison to my little girl obsession with the portrait of the *Queen of the West.*

Every Saturday morning Dale Evans and Roy Rogers appeared on our small black and white television. The couple captured my attention. I cheered as the hero, Roy, rounded up and turned the outlaws over to the local sheriff. With the town's people safe from evil, Roy and Dale rode off into the sunset.

Dale Evans started her career as a singer. A screen test resulted in a movie role. She starred opposite John Wayne in a movie that featured her vocal talents. Inspired by the stage musical, *Oklahoma,* Herbert Yates (head of Republic Studios) decided to expand the female role in westerns. He reasoned because Dale was from Texas, she should be able to ride and rope. Her Texas roots failed to guarantee her abilities as a cowgirl. She learned to ride on the set with the help of Roy and the Wranglers. The couple starred in twenty-eight Republic films. By the 1950s, they owned the production company and captivated young television audiences.

When my idols visited Abilene for a March of Dimes telethon, Dale Evans sought the expertise of *The Cowboy*

Hairstylist. I stared with rapt attention at the image of the beautiful actress. Every episode ended with Dale and Roy riding away on Buttermilk and Trigger. My only riding experience occurred when the traveling photographer sat me on his pony long enough to take a picture. Still, I dreamed of disappearing over the horizon as I sang *Happy Trails to You.*

Mr. and Mrs. Scoggins managed three successful businesses; the downtown Windsor Hotel Beauty Corral, a salon in the new mall, and an Academy that trained future hairstylists. Mother attended Scoggins' Beauty Academy. More than the essentials of cosmetology, she learned professional ethics and developed skills that served her throughout her career. After graduation, Mr. Scoggins hired her to work at the Windsor Corral.

Though the photo gallery mesmerized me, it wasn't my favorite part of visits to the salon. The coke machine fascinated me. My parents rarely bought sodas. Purchasing a soda rewarded good behavior. When I preformed up to my mother's standards, she doled out a nickel and a penny. I inserted the coins in the slots, lifted the soda from the top, and used the machine's opener to remove the cap. I savored the icy cold liquid – an exceptional treat.

When Mr. Scoggins closed the Windsor Hotel location, mother purchased the furniture and equipment. She opened Wanda's Salon of Beauty on Grape Street. The best treasure of all – the coke machine came with us.

Wanda's Salon of Beauty

"Hairdressers are a wonderful breed. You work one-on-one with another human being and the object is to make them feel so much better, and to look at themselves with a twinkle in their eye."
Vidal Sassoon

"Mom, it's really burning. I can't stand it," I cried.

My urgent pleas caught Mom's attention. She'd bleached my hair dozens of times with no more than some minor irritation. Years as the daughter of a beautician, who showed no patience for tender headed whiners, taught me to endure pain. The fiery sensation warned me not to remain silent. "Wash it off, now!" I howled.

Something in my tone caused Mom to move quickly. She washed off the chemical, but not before it scalded my entire scalp. One huge blister covered the top of my head. The failed experiment ended bleach and toner for me. I wisely decided - blonde-haired girls did not have enough fun to endure that kind of pain.

"You can't expect to sell beauty if you don't look good," my mother advised her employees.

She never left the house without full make-up, manicured fingernails, and perfectly styled hair. She expected the same of her daughters, especially the firstborn. She believed my appearance reflected her abilities and considered my hairstyle an advertisement for the salon. . Every morning before I went to school, she teased and styled my sixties bouffant to the perfect flip or an up-do of sculpted curls. To my surprise and dismay, I graduated from high school, got married, and moved three hours away with an inability to style my own hair.

Mother experimented with every new product and the newest styles. I happily complied. Through my teen years, I sported hair of every color. While my friends considered the beauty salon a treat, I lived there. Most afternoons, Mom picked me up from school. If she couldn't break away, I walked to the salon. After a short rest, I busied myself with chores. I washed and sterilized the tools of the trade – permanent rods, rollers, brushes, and combs. Beauticians of the sixties re-used everything to save money. The pungent odor of permanent wave solution signaled my least favorite task. The distinctive smell meant a wad of papers waited for me to wash, straighten, and stack neatly. I

Yellow Pages Listing

much preferred the task of loading the soda machine, since a cold drink rewarded completion of the assignment.

Mom took pride in her profession. She knew the value of a good haircut, the chemistry of color, and could roll a permanent in record time. She perfected multitasking before anyone recognized the ability. While one customer's perm processed, she rolled or pin-curled another. One woman sat under the drier, while another waited in the chair for a comb-out.

All the while, the ladies shared stories of their lives and the latest gossip of the town. The clientele exemplified a cross section of Abilene's population. A trip to the salon represented the one luxury an average woman allowed herself. The regulars knew each other well and freely shared details of their lives.

Mother's creativity shined when she experimented on my hair. Trade magazines, shows, and competitions displayed the current trends. A shy teenager, I never called attention to myself. However, I loved being the girl with the latest trendy style. I willingly allowed her to try the latest techniques. When Mom worked on my hair, she focused on me, just me. At home, I shared her attention with my siblings. None of us commanded her undivided attention.

Our family rarely traveled and never stayed in upscale hotels. When Mom announced, "I signed up for a hairstyle workshop/competition in Dallas. Would you like to be my model?"

Would I? Really? Seriously? I get to skip school. Just Mom and Me. We'll stay in a hotel. Of course, I want to go! When do we leave! Thoughts raced through my mind. I could hardly contain the excitement as I calmly answered, "Sure, it could be fun."

Mom lectured me about the practice required over the next few weeks. I agreed to let her cut my hair at the show if necessary. All the rules spelled out, we made plans for the competition and the trip to Dallas.

Everything about the trip exceeded my wildest dreams. Wide-eyed, I took in every opulent detail of the historic hotel. In 1912, Dallas city leaders approached St.

Louis beer baron Adolphus Busch to build a luxury hotel. Over the years, the twenty-one story baroque styled structure continued to offer an elegant, sophisticated charm.

Though as a teenager, I failed to appreciate the architecture and the historic impact of The Hotel Adolphus, I recognized its elegance.

Beyond our luxurious surroundings, I recognized the extraordinary opportunity the workshop afforded. Vidal Sassoon emerged as a celebrity – a trendsetter – renowned artist of the 1960s. The tradeshow participants learned the new technique and each model sported the fashionable new "Sassoon" haircut.

I instinctively knew the importance of this place and this event. The significance of the weekend far exceeded the opulence of the hotel or the celebrity of the renowned hairstylist. I spent the entire weekend with my mother. My insecurities took the weekend off –

Wanda Juanita Carr Dooly Miller

I felt special, pretty, and important. Sporting a trendsetting hairstyle, I returned to Abilene feeling confident and fashionable.

"There is no such thing as natural beauty."
Truvy in Steel Magnolias by Robert Harling

The Joy of Creation

"A man who works with his hands is a laborer;
a man who works with his hands and his brain is a craftsman;
but a man who works with his hands
and his brain and his heart is an artist."
Louis Nizer

"The dress will be ready before the baby arrives," Mother assured me.

I watched as she carefully constructed each piece. She added stiff boning to give shape to the red lace over satin bodice. "Stand still." Mom chided as she pinned the garment on my petite frame. "I'll add a stiff petticoat so the gathered skirt will stand out."

I stood like a statue. Experience taught me not to move. The slightest movement resulted in stabbing pain as the straight pins pierced my tender flesh. My first formal dress took shape. "It's beautiful. I look like a princess."

Nine months pregnant, my mother sewed feverishly. She overcame her tendency for procrastination, because she understood something beyond my comprehension. Once her fourth child arrived, the demands on her energy and attention would leave little time for sewing.

The evening for the banquet arrived. I stood beside the piano in the church fellowship hall facing the banquet guests. I lacked the good sense to be nervous. Well prepared by months of practice, multiple times each day, I sang *Winter Wonder Land,* the lyrics permanently ingrained in my mind. The cuteness factor of a nine year old with enough confidence to sing for a crowd impressed the audience. They encouraged me regardless of any talent I might or might not possess. No matter how I performed, they loved me, and I knew it.

Mom beamed with pride. "That's my girl! Didn't she do well?"

She responded to inquiries of, "Where did you find that darling dress?"

"Oh I didn't buy it. I made it. Yes, it is lovely. It turned out quite well."

The little red party dress bolstered Mom's confidence in her sewing abilities. I never doubted her ability to make anything my sisters and I imagined. "I like the bodice from this pattern, the sleeves from another, and the collar from yet another."

"I think this might work better," she suggested. "If it doesn't work, we'll try something else."

The white dress for my GA Coronation served as practice for the wedding dresses she designed for my sister and me. Bridal party attire proved simple compared to the more formal gowns.

Economic constraints necessitated sewing for our household. Though Mom really enjoyed sewing, often our needs and projects kept her up late at night after long, grueling workdays. If we suggested a store bought alternative she replied, "I can make a much better dress for less money."

Unlike the obligatory projects for her daughters, Mom found new joy in creating outfits for her first granddaughter. She delighted in dressing the little girl in frills and lace. Utilizing remnants, she celebrated the ability to make something that cost almost nothing.

With scraps from Lisa's drill team uniform, she created a miniature uniform for the toddler to wear to her aunt's football games. The preschooler rewarded her grandmother's efforts with squeals of pleasure at each new creation. Grammer played dress-up with her little model. It was hard to tell who enjoyed the game more.

As the girl grew to a young lady, she learned what her mother already knew. *Grammer can sew anything I need or want to wear.*

"Grammer, I need a dress for the journalism banquet and a different one for the choir banquet. Oh, I'd really like something special for my piano recital. If Mom buys the material, will you make them? You know how hard it is for me to find store bought dresses that fit right." the teenager bargained.

A trip to the fabric store ensued. The search for the material and elements to create an original design provided as much excitement as the finished product.

Mother loved to sew. It provided an emotional outlet. She exuded talent and lost herself in the creative process. She enjoyed the challenge of combining elements and personalizing each creation. She prided herself in designing something unique. "No one else will have anything like yours," She proudly announced.

During a visit one afternoon, Mom asked, "Could you take pictures of Ginger in the dresses I've made? I want to make a photo album."

Her short-lived idea of making formals for profit fell flat. After the first commission, she realized sewing for money failed to produce the same joy as creating a masterpiece for the children she adored.

Mom perfected her sewing techniques and never accepted less than exceptional quality. She took great pride in figuring out the complexities of difficult patterns. She poured her heart and stitched love into each garment. After all, she created it for someone she loved. Each project became a work of art, not hanging in a gallery – instead it adorned her most precious gifts – her daughters and granddaughters.

Sibling Rivalry

"I don't believe an accident of birth makes people sisters or brothers. It makes them siblings, gives them mutuality of parentage. Sisterhood and brotherhood is a condition people have to work at."
Maya Angelou

"Wanda Merle, don't you hurt that baby!" Momo screeched.

Mike ran to the bedroom, shook the bed frame, and grabbed the loosened slat. He used any available weapon to equalize our size. He threatened me with the one by four piece of wood, as the three of us ran through the house. I evaded potential strikes as I looked for the opportunity to disarm him. "Hurt him? I'm just trying to defend myself!"

The sight resembled something from a bad comic movie. I dodged and weaved in a well-defined path evading both the furniture and my brother. Momo followed close behind in an attempt to minimize any potential damage to her favored grandson. She hated the constant arguments and felt helpless to stop the physical confrontations. Neither of us heeded her pleas.

"You're not the boss of me. I don't have to do what you say," Mike yelled and defied my perceived authority.

"I'm calling Mother," I reached the phone and dialed the familiar number to the beauty salon.

"Let me talk to him," Mom responded angrily.

I handed the phone to my brother and waited as she threatened delayed consequences when she got home. He handed the phone back to me. "She wants to talk to you."

"If you call me at work again, there better be blood," she scolded me harshly.

Deflated, I hung up the phone. The physical threat neutralized, I retrieved the bed-slat and returned it to the proper place supporting my mattress. I suppressed the hot tears that threatened to spill from my eyes. *I'll never let him see me cry.*

The fear of punishment stopped my brother's pursuit and the physical threat. Unfortunately, the hostility remained.

We retreated to separate parts of the house. None of us recalled the cause of the fight. Mike played with his toys. Momo returned to her routine chores. I collapsed on my bed contemplating Mother's reprimand. Her disappointed tone stung. *What does she want from me? I should be hanging out with my friends not taking care of my siblings. I'm a teenager not an adult. Nothing I do pleases her.*

By the time Mother arrived home, the rest of the family slept. None of us ever discussed the conflict.

My parents frequently left me in charge of my younger siblings. My brother and I argued frequently. Eventually, experience taught us to resolve our differences without resorting to violence. I wisely decided to relinquish any attempt to control his behavior, and we learned to co-exist.

Discipline of my younger sisters proved less challenging. Close in age, the girls usually played well together. They typically settled their differences amicably. Lisa, the more passive child, generally acquiesced to the stronger will of her three older siblings. A decade older, my size provided a distinct advantage when the situation required a position of authority. Occasionally contentious arguments persisted and necessitated an intervention.

When requiring the pair to apologize, hug, and kiss each other failed to resolve the squabble, I sought another solution. I drew inspiration from a Bible story. In my youthful understanding, I misinterpreted the story of Jesus washing the disciples' feet. However, the passage inspired me, and I conceived an idea to deal with my sister's sibling rivalry.

The next time an argument erupted, I seized the opportunity to test my theory. When the usual methods to contain the fight failed, I collected my sisters. "Take off your shoes."

They looked at me with puzzled faces, "Why?"

"You'll see," I replied.

When they protested, I helped them remove their shoes. "Now, kiss each other's feet."

"Yuk, no way! Her feet stink!" they objected.

The first experience proved successful. They kissed each other's feet. With the task completed, we all giggled and forgot the cause of the original argument. I celebrated the success of my parenting skills.

The experiment's positive effect proved temporary and before long, another argument presented a chance to utilize the unique method of discipline. The next time I gathered the girls during a quarrel, they knew what to expect. "No way! Not again! That's nasty. Her feet smell horrible!"

My persistence paid off. They obediently, if reluctantly, removed their shoes. Lisa went first. She compliantly kissed Patty's feet. When Patty knelt, instead of kissing her baby sister's feet, she spit on them. She immediately shot out the front door and ran down the street. I grabbed a plastic fly swatter and chased her through the neighborhood. When I finally caught her, I popped her bottom. To my horror, the plastic cracked and broke into two pieces. The fight ended abruptly with a heartfelt apology. The punishment affected me much more than my younger sister.

I continued to use this technique as my preferred discipline method to control arguments between my sisters. It worked so well that Lisa employed it with her own daughters. Her four girls found the practice disgusting and credit this practice with their foot phobias.

Unless you grew up as an only child, memories of sibling rivalry comprise some of our most dramatic and sometimes comical childhood stories. As adults, we recall the stories and laugh at our shared experiences.

Fortunately, we outgrew the need to control each other. We understand the idiosyncrasies of our shared history. Because we recognize and appreciate our differences, we enjoy being together. I seldom feel the need to explain myself to my siblings, though I openly share my heart with them.

An accident of birth provided me with a family of amazing siblings. Our commitment to love and support each other bonded us as lifelong friends.

A Tender Young Heart

"But if you find yourself experiencing a desire to seek God, we have great news for you: God is already at work in you."
Henry T. Blackaby,
Experiencing the Spirit: The Power of Pentecost Every Day

Are we there yet? How much further? Where are we? Though the restless pre-teens wondered, no one dared ask aloud. Our parents raised us to politely follow directions and quietly obey adults in authority. The little more than one-hour distance seemed much longer to the anxious girls. *Will we ever get there? I really need to go to the bathroom.*

Finally, the station wagon pulled through the gate, stopped at the registration area. The driver killed the motor, and rolled down the windows. "Stay here, while I go in and register our group. I'll be back in a minute," our sponsor instructed.

When she returned, we continued to our assigned cabin. "Here we are," she announced as she opened the car door, and released the captives.

Dozens of girls chattered at the same time. Each girl excitedly staked her territory for the week. "Let's get our cots next to each other! We want the ones close to the screens – away from the walls!"

Cots lined both sides of the open room. Screened-in porches surrounded the central room reserved for the counselors. Experienced sponsors brought large box fans to provide a breeze over their own cots. The cabins offered few of the comforts of home – no air, simple toilets, and community showers. The more experienced campers sought bunks near the corners to take advantage of the nightly breezes. The corner bunks offered an additional benefit of distance from the counselors so the girls could chat and share secrets late into the night.

The items brought from home revealed the girls understanding of the stringent rules. Each camper adhered to the list of prohibited items. No transistor radios, no short-shorts, or hot- pants, nothing to distract us from the camp's spiritual purpose. None of the well-disciplined girls considered challenging the established traditions. The dress code forbade two-piece swimsuits and required cover-ups to walk from the cabin to the pool. A long held custom strictly enforced no *mixed bathing* - boys and girls swam at different times. Girls dressed modestly in *Bermuda length shorts* or *peddle-pushers.*

A mid-afternoon break allowed respite from the Texas summer heat. Before dinner, we freshened up and dressed for evening worship service in the tabernacle. The gathering concluded the camper's day and required the same decorum as attending church. As a sign of reverence, girls wore dresses or skirts and blouses.

Lueders, Texas provided a secluded rural setting on the Clear Fork of the Brazos. The solitary location offered isolation from life's daily distractions. Lueders Baptist Encampment served generations of West Texas area youth. Baptist history reports the first camp occurred July 12-14, 1898. Young people from Haskell, Albany, Anson, and Abilene met in a beautiful pecan grove on the Clear Fork for a "season of physical and spiritual refreshing." (A

Centennial History of Texas Baptists, Broadman Press, 1936)

The charter members of the 1898 group voted to form a permanent organization under the name of West Texas Baptist Union. Later the name would change to Lueders Baptist Encampment. In 1973, Big Country Baptist Assembly adopted its current name. Founded by Christian youth for Christian youth, the camp continues to provide a rural retreat venue. Supported by documentation in newspaper clippings, photos, and even a Baptist seminary history textbook, many believe the BCBA may be the oldest continuing Christian Youth Camp in the world.

GA Camp at Lueders introduced me to Southern Baptist Missions. I listened with rapt attention to the stories of the missionaries and the children they served. I loved the pictures of the people in far away villages. The stories of the medical missionaries especially captured my heart.

As a six-year-old child, I opened my heart and asked Jesus to save me. Initially, I understood Christ as Savior and trusted Him to save me from my sin and give me eternal life. As a child, I heard many sermons on the reality of hell and knew I wanted to avoid the destination. Experiences at GA camp sowed seeds of growth and deepened my personal relationship with God. My lifelong spiritual journey began.

I loved Lueders! One week, each summer of my pre-teen years, my peers and I focused on the basic concepts necessary for a firm spiritual foundation. The retreat offered freedom from responsibilities of caring for my younger siblings. We swam every day – a rare treat! Activities, crafts, and Bible study occupied our days. The worship assembly deepened my love for music and taught me to listen for God's voice.

My most enduring memory of the camp experience occurred on the last night of camp. Instead of the worship service in the Tabernacle, we met on the banks of the Clear Fork of the Brazos River. I listened as the camp pastor spoke of Christ's sacrifice for me. The minister encouraged us to speak directly to God. "Take one of these cards and write a message. It may be asking God to forgive your sins. Perhaps, you need to surrender some area of your life to Him. Whatever your need – this is between you and God."

A campfire and the moonlight illuminated a cross on the opposite bank of the river. The camp pastor encouraged us to focus on a personal relationship with God. During my rebellious teen years, the compelling image of Christ's sacrifice convicted me. Even when I pulled away from the church, I recognized God's presence.

During quiet moments at camp, I experienced God's call to serve Him with my life. As a young girl, I thought the calling directed me to medical missions. I knew one thing clearly – God had a purpose for my life. In the more than five decades since my camp experience, I found God to be faithful even when I wasn't. Though I took an unconventional education and career path, I found my true calling.

My call to missions played itself out in an entirely unexpected way. For six years, I worked with the Girls in Action mission organization in our Dallas church. We met weekly, participated in mission activities, and attended associational events including GA camp at Mount Lebanon in Cedar Hill, Texas. Encounters at Mount Lebanon stirred memories of my own camp experiences at Lueders.

God allowed me to work with and encourage girls who sought His will for their lives. My GA students followed God's calling for their lives – several as teachers – one social worker – others in the business community – two as Southern Baptist Missionaries. Years later, one of these young missionaries assured me. "See, Wanda, we really did pay attention."

Though I detoured, God never gave up on me. The seeds planted and the scriptures written on my heart built a foundation on which I based my life.

Growing in Grace
Learning to Listen

"Arise; shine for thy light is come."
Isaiah 60:1

One week each year, I attended a camp focused on missions. The missionaries' pictures and vivid accounts of their lives in foreign countries captivated me. I understood God loved me and had a plan for my life. My tender heart responded. From the time I was a little girl, I wanted to be a nurse. I committed my life to God and planned to serve Him as a medical missionary.

I dedicated myself to learning about missions and missionaries. Every Wednesday evening, we went to GAs. I joined the generations of girls who participated in mission's education and hands-on mission involvement. The Women's Missionary Union of the Southern Baptist Convention formed Girls Auxiliary in 1913 to encourage girls and young women to help others in Jesus' name.

Perhaps I participated in the Forward Steps program because I loved the idea of being a part of the coronation that declared me first a maiden, then a lady-in-waiting, a princess and finally a Queen.

The structured program encouraged us to memorize scripture and grow spiritually. The scripture I learned established a firm foundation. These verses sustained, and comforted me during the most difficult seasons of my life.

As a little girl, I worked hard to complete the requirements for each step. I participated in the recognition services being a part of the queenly court of my older friends. Finally, it was my turn. My mother and my leaders planned the details of my coronation. I felt regal in the white satin dress embellished with hand-sewn white pearls at the neckline. Matching satin covered my crown and pearls accented its tips. My spirited little brother fulfilled his obligation, behaving properly as the courtly crown bearer. He walked down the aisle as instructed and practiced. Carrying my crown on a satin pillow, he stood erect until the leader removed the crown and placed it on my head. The celebratory reception followed the traditional ceremony.

Queen Jamie Lacy's Coronation –I'm on the far left, Princess Wanda.

During my high school years, I drifted away from my spiritual commitment. I abandoned my plan to become a medical missionary. Life took unexpected turns, and a college education seemed unattainable. I graduated from high school and married two weeks later, deserting my dream of a nursing career.

As a young girl with a tender, open heart, I experienced a desire to follow Christ. Because of this commitment, God revealed His purpose for my life. Though I often fell short of His example and my own expectations, He continued to work in and through me. He clearly directed me to health care, and I eventually earned my nursing credentials. Ultimately, I followed my true calling to nursing, specifically to oncology nursing. My position allowed me to show God's love to hurting patients and caregivers. What a privilege!

Bargain Matinee
An Afternoon of Dreams for Fifty Cents

"Everything I learned, I learned from the movies."
Audrey Hepburn

"Hurry up! Let's finish our chores so we can go to the movie," I prompted my little brother.

Our desire to spend Saturday afternoon at The Metro with our friends united us in an effort to finish the necessary tasks. I hurried through my responsibilities and picked out a cute outfit. I wanted to look good in case my latest crush showed up at the theater. "Come on. We're going to be late," my younger brother, less concerned about his appearance, pulled me out the door.

I secured a one-dollar bill and ran out the door to meet the neighborhood kids who waited at the curb. We mounted our bikes and rode the two miles to the theater. We arrived at the theater just before the feature started and stood in line to purchase our tickets. Fifty cents purchased one ticket to the movie. We rarely possessed money to purchase concessions. Once inside, I found my girl friends and located seats as far away from my brother as possible. I occupied the same seat for the entire afternoon always watching the movie at least twice and sometimes a third time.

James Griffin designed the Quonset hut styled Metro Theater and located all 526 wooden seats on the main floor. Behind the brick façade, a vestibule housed the attraction sign, lobby, ticket area, and projection booth. Just prior to opening, the I.B. Adleman circuit purchased the building and launched the theater on October 17, 1946 with the film, "Ding Dong Williams." The next few years proved rocky and the business closed in 1949.

Six months later the theater re-launched and found its audience. Marketing to the students at nearby McMurry College, it featured popular priced runs of films like "The Ten Commandments" and "Ben Hur." The Metro continued to serve the clientele of southern Abilene for over thirty years.

Saturday afternoon movie matinees provided escape from the ordinary. For a few hours, I experienced total freedom from responsibility. I forgot schoolwork and the pressure to perform. Someone else cared for my siblings. I imagined myself as the heroine in the cowboy flick, the glamorous starlet, the singer, the dancer, or the princess. Every week I assumed a different starring role.

Movies introduced my generation to John Wayne, The Lone Ranger, Roy Rogers, and Dale Evans. The cowboy films taught us to expect good to triumph over evil.

Gregory Peck raised our consciousness in "To Kill a Mockingbird." "Peter Pan" encouraged us never to grow up. Disney movies encouraged our fantasy belief in happily ever after.

The innocence of the early sixties afforded a measure of independence to the baby boomer generation. When I proved my ability to act responsibly, my parents rewarded me with additional freedom. Our parents allowed us to ride our bikes or walk wherever we wanted to go. I followed my parent's one rule – be home before dark. No problem, by that time, our empty stomachs begged for food.

Movies and books helped me use fantasy as a healthy coping mechanism. Drama and literature allowed me to experience a world beyond my reality. I found a release for bottled up emotions. Escaping reality into a world of possibilities encouraged me to reach for my dreams. It still does.

A Short Lived Seamstress Career

"If you can design one thing, you can design everything."
Massimo Vignelli

"The American Wool Council sponsors an annual competition for students in several categories. The Make It with Wool contest encourages creativity in sewing, knitting, crocheting, spinning, weaving, and other needlework art. Students in Texas schools compete against each other. The winner receives a scholarship. If you decide to enter, you may use the garment as your class project, and you will earn extra credit," Ms. Smith announced to our home economics class as she distributed papers detailing rules for the contest.

Never one to turn down extra credit, I listened intently as the teacher provided additional details. "Participants must select, construct, accessorize, and model their own garments."

When Mom picked me up from school, I excitedly waved the paper in her face. "Look, Mom! We can do this!"

"There's no we in these rules," she responded. "You have to do this on your own."

"I know," I replied. "But you can supervise. It will be fun."

My mother could make any garment I dreamed up. *Surely, I inherited the ability to construct a garment. If I run into difficulty, she'll be able to talk me through it,* I thought. When Mother finished work, we walked to Cloth World, the fabric store located across the street from the beauty salon.

"You need something different – a unique pattern – something not everyone else will choose," Mom definitely was on board.

We directed our attention to the Vogue pattern books, bypassing the Simplicity and Butterick areas. We never considered my status as a beginner. I chose a two-piece suit, with a trendy A-line skirt and matching jacket. We selected royal blue lightweight wool fabric. Mom held up the fabric to my face. "This is a perfect color for you. It emphasizes the color of your eyes."

We chose material to line the suit, a skirt zipper, and extravagantly priced buttons. With our purchase completed, we headed home.

I lacked the experience to doubt my ability to complete the project. I confidently began by trimming each pattern piece and carefully following the specific directions exactly as printed. I soon realized the complexity of my suit. *Really, this suit has a waistband, a zipper, a collar, buttons, buttonholes – and it's fully lined. What was I thinking! As much as I want to quit, I'm committed. Mom spent a small fortune for the supplies. I can't give up.*

Each night when Mom came home from work, she inspected my work. The zipper caused the seams of my skirt to pucker, and the lining didn't line up. "Tear it out and do it over," Mom instructed.

I repeated the process and did my best to correct the mistakes and measure up to my mother's perfectionist standards. Tiny holes in the wool evidenced each mistake. Every attempt resulted in a torrent of tears and feelings of failure. I desperately wanted Mom to rescue my disaster. "Please, please just fix it," I pleaded.

"You know, I can't do that. The rules say it has to be your creation." She wouldn't budge.

I no longer cared about the contest. I simply wanted to be finished.

The deadline for submission loomed. Several sleepless nights – Finally, though far from perfect – we called it done. I presented it to the owner of the dry cleaner's establishment next door to Mother's beauty salon. I desperately hoped that a professional pressing would improve the overall presentation of my suit.

"You did a really nice job. You'll look beautiful in it," the motherly owner of the dry cleaners encouraged me as she handed back the completed garment.

"Thank you," I beamed as I responded politely. "A professional pressing made it look so much better."

Accessorizing proved to be far more fun. I needed shoes, a hat, and gloves not available at the five and dime or at either Clark's or Gibson's Discount Stores. We rarely shopped Minter's downtown department store, whose prices typically exceeded our budget. Excitedly, I embarked on my mission and found a helpful saleslady, "I need to find a hat to compliment my suit. I'll be modeling it in the Make It with Wool Contest."

She matched my enthusiasm and helped me try on every hat in the store. "Try this winter white leather – it provides a nice contrast to the royal blue. Matching white kid leather gloves will give you a polished look."

She placed the bubble style hat with a snuggly fitting white band and silver buckle accent on my head. "I love it. It reminds me of something Twiggy would wear. It's perfect."

The face of 1966, Twiggy, a London born model, became the first international supermodel and exemplified the sixties look. Teenage girls incorporated a little of Twiggy's look in their own personal style.

"Why don't you try on the entire outfit and get the full effect?" the saleslady encouraged.

I gazed into the mirror, pleased with the overall look. When I stepped out of the dressing room, Mother and the sales clerk bolstered my confidence with their approving nods.

Mom paid for the twenty-five dollar hat and the gloves from her salon's daily cash receipts.

I modeled my creation in the style show a week later. Though my suit won no awards, I wore it proudly. The suit remained in my wardrobe until I could no longer squeeze my body into it.

The experience pushed me beyond my comfort zone. I put aside my normally shy manner and confidently took center stage. When I wanted to quit, I persevered and completed the project. With all its flaws, I accepted the imperfections and took pride in my accomplishment. I failed to discover a love for sewing and realized the lack of an inherited sewing ability. If a sewing gene exists, it definitely skipped my DNA.

Fifty years later, the vintage white leather hat remains at the top of my closet in its original Minter's Department Store box, a tangible reminder of valuable lessons resulting from a high school home economics project.

Flight of a Reticent Butterfly

"Just when the caterpillar thought the world was over –
it became a butterfly."
Edward Teller

I read the invitation and examined the envelope to verify its intended recipient. The name and address belonged to me. It appeared genuine.

THE SOUTHWEST ABILENE ROTARY CLUB
REQUESTS THE HONOR OF YOUR PRESENCE
AS ONE OF THE TOP FIFTY SENIOR STUDENTS
OF THE ABILENE PUBLIC HIGH SCHOOLS
CLASS OF SIXTY EIGHT - SIXTY NINE
TUESDAY, MAY THIRTEENTH AT SEVEN-THIRTY P.M.
AT THE
McGLOTHLIN CAMPUS CENTER
ABILENE CHRISTIAN COLLEGE
REPLY IF DECLINING
INFORMAL DRESS
PRESENT INVITATION AT THE DOOR

The class ranks listed my name as twenty-four in a graduating class of just over five hundred. I enthusiastically squealed as I bounced through the empty house wishing for someone to celebrate the achievement. *I can't wait for Mother and Daddy to get home from work. I hope they'll be surprised and proud. Looks like all the studying and hard work paid off.*

Though I continued to focus on completing necessary assignments to earn a high school diploma, I spent most of my time dreaming about my upcoming wedding. Details of the wedding usurped normal high school graduation activities. Nothing about high school excited me – at least so I thought. The elated reaction to the invitation I held in my hand disproved my professed indifference. *I really did it! I earned this!*

Informal dress – What does that mean? What should I wear? My wedding shower dress should be finished soon. It will work fine.

Mom expertly sewed every one of my special occasion outfits. Each evening she frantically worked on the dresses for every wedding event. The beautiful spring floral dress she created for my wedding shower equaled any store bought fashion my classmates might choose. The dress assured confidence in my appearance – helping me overcome my natural shyness.

Closer inspection of the card changed my mood from euphoria to desolation. No doubt, I earned my place at the banquet. I checked and re-checked the date. Who plans a banquet on a school night in the middle of the week? No mistake – May thirteenth. *Maybe I'm wrong about the date of the Austin trip.* I hurried to the bedroom and dug out the confirmatory letter. The document clearly stated the schedule for my cosmetology state exam. Written exam scheduled for Monday, May 12th, with the practical exam the following morning. By the time the bus returned to Abilene, the banquet would be over.

How could I complete the test in Austin and still receive recognition for my academic accomplishments? I yearned for a solution. Salty tears rolled down my cheeks. The silent tears escalated to sobs. I threw myself across the bed and wept bitterly. Tears spent and physically exhausted, I finally sat up, dried my eyes, and decided to call Mom.

I shuffled through the house to the phone in the hallway. I dialed the number to my mother's beauty salon. I hoped she might solve my problem, or at least share the pain.

To my surprise and contrary to her normal demeanor, she remained quite calm. The situation presented a challenge but not an insurmountable one.

My mother always arrived late. Her disorganized approach wreaked havoc on my need for order. Contrary to her usual helter-skelter approach, she took charge. Over the next few days, Mom arranged for transportation and connections. The plan hinged on perfect timing and detailed preparation.

On Sunday afternoon, I traveled on the bus with my classmates to Austin. As scheduled, on Monday morning we took the written portion of our state exam. The following morning we arrived at the testing center to demonstrate the skills we learned in class over the past two years. The test required us to show our expertise on partners. We shampooed each other's hair, rolled a section of hair on permanent rods. Finally, we placed finger waves and pin curls in each other's hair.

As soon as the test administrator released us, I dashed to a waiting taxi, which drove me to the airport. I covered my pin-curled hair with a stylish feathery cap, expecting my wet hair to dry naturally on the flight home. I boarded the airplane. I rarely traveled and certainly never flew. I anxiously awaited take off. The short flight arrived in Abilene on schedule. *Perfect plan coming together.*

Being a very talented hairstylist, Mom planned to use her skills to transform my pin-curled, finger-waved hair to a masterpiece. Her plan included brushing, teasing and sweeping it into an up-do. Unfortunately, we encountered a glitch in the plan. Mom never anticipated soaking wet curls. I dressed in the airport bathroom. Ever resourceful, Mom pulled my hair up into a tight bun and plopped a pre-styled wiglet on top of my wet head. The dress and hair passed inspection.

I miraculously arrived on time to Abilene Christian College where I attended the Rotary Club event recognizing the achievements of the class of 1969.

The self-absorbed teenager in me never realized how much my parents sacrificed to make that evening possible. Like Edward Tiller's caterpillar, I thought my world was over. I saw only an impossible situation. However, with my parents' support I emerged like the butterfly to celebrate and soar.

Meet Me at Mack's

"Quick! Hang a right – Cut over to G Street. I just saw a vision! I saw a goddess. Come on, You've got to catch up to her – This was the most perfect, dazzling creature I've ever seen – She spoke to me. She spoke to me right through the window. I think she said, "I love you." That means nothing to you people? You have no romance, no soul? She – someone wants me. Someone roaming the streets wants me! Will you turn the corner?"
Curt Henderson, Movie quote from American Graffiti.

The summer of 2009 found me eagerly anticipating my fortieth class reunion. My eagerness to attend all the events surprised me. Over the years, I maintained contact with very few high school acquaintances. However, the social media site, Classmates.com, afforded the opportunity to reconnect with members of the Abilene High School class of '69. I found myself recalling pleasant memories as I thought about high school friends and acquaintances and wondered about their adult personalities. *I'm no longer the shy insecure teenager. I interact with all kinds of people on a daily basis. I have every reason to be proud of my accomplishments.* I encouraged myself as I carefully selected and packed clothes for the weekend.

The weekend started with the homecoming football game. The home team, 2009 state champions, led at half time by a score of 63–0.

One of the Eagle's class of '69 football players quipped, "I played football all through high school. I don't think we scored a total of 63 points the entire three years."

Everyone around him laughed as we remembered the dismal win/loss records of our high-school teams. Despite the outcome, we remained loyal to our school and cheered for the team no matter the score. Certainly, we never contended for a state championship position.

The evening ended with a celebration of the current team's homecoming victory and a chorus of, "See you at Mack's tomorrow afternoon?"

"Absolutely! I'm looking forward to it."

The planned gathering promised an opportunity to recreate experiences of the baby boomer class. Alumni gathered at Arrow Ford's Loan Arranger for an afternoon of nostalgia. The owners preserved the classic feel and legacy of the property. Though the building served a completely different purpose, our memories of weekends spent on this block remained intact.

The Hollywood script for "American Graffiti" depicted scenes reminiscent of places like Mack Eplen's Drivateria on any given Friday or Saturday night during the late fifties, through the sixties and into the early seventies. The fictional Mel's Drive-in and the cruising strip in Modesto, California represented local teen hangouts in almost any town in America. Sixties slang defines cruising as driving up and down the strip, street or town looking for members of the opposite sex. For kids growing up in Abilene, Mack's provided that place – a rite of passage.

The reunion committee welcomed alumni of the AHS class of '69 to an afternoon of the restaurant's signature pink cookies and sharing memories of the iconic site. We opened a treasure chest of memories. Whether alone, with a date, or a carload of friends, everyone eventually ended up at Mack's every Friday and Saturday evening.

One wise guy cracked, "They served food? We just cruised – clockwise for a while, then counterclockwise so you didn't miss anyone."

The tradition of circling allowed guys to show off cars – sometimes the new shiny one he borrowed from dad for the night – another, lucky enough to own a hot sports car – for the mechanically inclined, the pride and joy of a restoration work in progress. Some cruisers pulled into parking spots, actually ordered, and spotted friends as they drove by. "We burned lots of fuel every weekend. Fortunately, gas prices averaged eighteen cents a gallon."

The girls spent hours on make-up and the perfect bouffant hairstyle. Once satisfied with our look, a group of friends piled into a car and headed to Mack's. Someone recalled, "I remember cruising the block. When we stopped at the stop signs, someone yelled, 'Chinese fire drill' and the passengers all jumped out and ran around the car before proceeding to the next leg of the route."

Mack's menu highlighted a Mexican plate for $1 and quarter-pound square burgers for 40 cents, with an extra nickel for cheese, and 35 cents more if you wanted fries. I rarely ordered anything from the menu except an occasional coke or dessert treat, the legendary pink cookie. My job at the Chuck Wagon offered the Friday night special of six burgers for a dollar. After making dozens of burgers and eating during my shift, Mack's hamburgers failed to tempt me. Resisting a pink cookie or brownie was much harder.

The food and beverages supplied the excuse, but social interactions provided the real reason to inch single file around the full city block.

"Mack's was our place to hang out in the '60s -- good food and a great place to see friends and make new ones. Does anyone else remember the '66 senior class stunt? They left class, walked, rather than driving, around Mack's." one person recalled.

"Remember our class stunt? We beat them all," another boasted. "One by one, we removed the knives from the school cafeteria. By the time the staff missed the knives, we'd collected most of them. One classmate's father, a local jeweler, engraved the knives with 'seniors '69'. The class presented a box of engraved knives to the vice-principal at our senior assembly. The administration failed to acknowledge or appropriately appreciate our gift."

Each time I left the house, regardless of my intended destination, I always detoured by Mack's. My younger sisters frequently rode with me in Dad's blue and white '57 Chevy. I introduced them to the Mack's experience. Since I feared the embarrassment of being seen with my siblings in tow, I forced them to duck down in the floorboard between the seats. I drove the pre-determined course and allowed them to sit back in the seats only when we cleared any possible cute boy sightings. I swore them to silence. "You can never tell Mom I took you to Mack's."

While I hid my sisters, my friend Monnie, employed an entirely different approach. "I took my mama driving around Mack's. If I found somebody (a guy) to ride around with, Mama could take the car home."

Carol scored the best prize of all. In 2016, she reminisced. "Well, I had been driving my standard Rambler around Mack's all afternoon. My foot went to sleep on the clutch. I let my friend, Brenda, drive. Her friend, David, jumped out of one car and into ours. We will be married forty-seven years in June."

Hollywood's "American Graffiti," "Broadway's Grease," and television's 'Happy Days' dramatize our experiences as we transitioned from high school to our adult lives. Some of the boys enlisted in the military and served our country in Vietnam. Many of my classmates pursued a college education. Others, including Monnie, Carol, and me, planned June weddings. The summer of 2016, all three couples celebrated our forty-seventh wedding anniversaries. We left behind adolescent practices but always treasured memories of carefree evenings when our biggest concerns focused on a date, a car, and enough gas to cruise Mack's.

On July 15, 2015, United Methodist Service Center and Pantry celebrated a grand opening at the site of the former drive-in restaurant. From the outside, the building looks much the same as when teens cruised the block, and carhops delivered burgers and fries directly to customers. Over the years occupants of the building preserved items from the days of Mack's, including a pale green carhop dress and vintage menus. The new owners honored the legacy of the building by researching and utilizing the original paint colors – blue and white.

The new use for the building on North 1st street reflects changing times. Older residents view the newly painted building with nostalgic eyes. However, the people standing in a long line out front, waiting for groceries to feed their families for a month, look at it with optimistic eyes. It seems fitting that a place dedicated to satisfying so many appetites over the years now provides food to families needing help and hope.

The inscription on the front of the building assures them they've come to the right place. The words of Jesus recorded in Matthew 25:35 affirm the agency's mission. "For I was hungry and you gave me food; I was thirsty and you gave me something to drink; I was a stranger and you invited me in."

United Methodist Service Center and Food Pantry –
Former Site of Mack Eplen's Drive-In. 2016

Mack Eplen's Pink Cookies and Icing
(as found on the internet)

1 c. powdered sugar
1 c. shortening
½ tsp. salt
¾ c. chopped pecans
1 egg
½ c. milk
1 tsp. salt
1 tsp. vanilla
½ tsp. lemon flavoring
4 c. cake flour

Icing:
¼ c. oil
¼ c. white corn syrup
1 Tbsp. water
pinch of salt
drop of cherry flavoring
drop of red food coloring
1 c. powdered sugar
½ tsp. milk

Mix all ingredients into a smooth paste. Roll into log shape and cut into
1-inch slices. Make an indentation in the center of each cookie by pressing
with thumb. Bake at 400 degrees for 10 minutes.

Icing: Bring oil, corn syrup, water, coloring and salt to a boil. Transfer it to
a mixing bowl. Add flavoring and sugar until it becomes a thick paste. Mix
until smooth. Add milk until icing reaches consistency to drop into
indentations in cookie. Let cool

Amusing Stories of Family Life Spouses - Siblings - Silliness

"I am convinced that most people do not grow up...We marry and dare to have children and call that growing up. I think what we do is mostly grow old. We carry accumulation of years in our bodies, and on our faces, but generally our real selves, the children inside, are innocent and shy as magnolias."

Maya Angelou, _Letter to My Daughter_

With This Ring

"With this Ring I thee wed, and with all my worldly goods I thee endow: In the Name of the Father, and of the Son, and of the Holy Ghost. Amen."
1789 Book of Common Prayer

"There are only two reasons why a man refuses to wear his wedding band." Wow! The minister suddenly commanded my undivided attention. "Either he is ashamed of his wife, or he desires to appear single."

My memory flashed back to a June afternoon in 1969.

Every detail of our small wedding screamed "sixties." Today I might claim a goal of simplicity, but truthfully, financial concerns determined every detail. The entire wedding cost less than $500, very different from the thousands of dollars spent on the average wedding in the twenty-first century.

My mother worked feverishly for months, designing and sewing not only my wedding gown, but also dresses for every female in the bridal party. She made her own mother-of-the-bride outfit as well as my dress for the rehearsal dinner. I slept while she sewed, blissfully unconcerned about the completion of the wedding party's attire.

The empire styled dresses typified the late sixties style. The attendants formed a pastel rainbow of blue, pink, and green dotted-Swiss. A brocade ribbon of daisies trimmed the bodice of the gowns, and matching hair bows held fresh daisies. White gloves and a single stem carnation completed the desired effect.

I never considered buying a wedding gown. Mom designed outfits for every major event in my life. I knew she could make anything I could dream up. Mother combined patterns to get the exact look I wanted. She painstakingly hand appliquéd Chantilly lace on the gown, the veil and the train. The wrist-length lace sleeves and high neck matched my introverted personality. The backless effect hinted at a daring side, well hidden until my wedding day.

Bridal magazines provided checklists for planning the event. This worked quite well for me. It felt strangely comforting to complete and cross off every detail suggested by the experts. Mother and her sisters arranged all aspects of the reception. Any anxiety over the details vanished as I prepared for my wedding day. In my mind, all bases were covered. I naively concerned myself with a daily routine that included writing a letter to my fiancée and graduating from high school, in that order. My youthful exuberance and immaturity blinded me to any unexpected disaster.

June 14, our wedding day finally arrived. Alone in my parent's bedroom, I admired Kerry's wedding band. *Worth every penny I paid for it!* My part-time job at the Chuck Wagon, a local hamburger joint, afforded a few dollars each week to retrieve the ring from layaway at the local jewelry store. The sentimental value of the small diamond set in white gold far outweighed the actual cost. I lovingly placed the ring in its small pouch, laid it on my parents' bed, and proceeded to dress for the most important day of my young life.

Everything at the church appeared perfect, exactly as I envisioned it. *Where's Kerry's Ring!* I escalated from cool, calm and collected to all out on the ceiling panic. I sent my matron-of-honor and soon to be sister-in-law, Karen, to find my daddy. *There's still plenty of time. He can go home and get the ring.* No problem. However, the panic soared when he returned to the church without the ring and calmly announced with his slow West Texas drawl, "I couldn't find it."

Karen took charge, "Go get Tommy's wedding band."

Wedding Party June 14, 1969

Daddy dutifully walked to the room where the guys waited for the ceremony to begin. He returned with the requested ring. My heart rate quickened and my palms began to sweat as my father and I entered the church. We marched down the aisle and joined my unsuspecting groom. We recited our vows and exchanged rings. I never dreamed the something borrowed for my wedding would be the groom's ring.

Contrasting photographs recorded the emotions of the day. The lens captured somber faces. Expressions of anxiety and uncertainty as my father and I walked down the aisle changed to portraits of relief and joy as newlyweds, Kerry and I left the church.

Before the reception began, I took care of unfinished business. I went immediately to the bedroom, retrieved the ring from its pouch, and placed it on my husband's left hand. I returned the borrowed ring to my brother-in-law.

Today, simple gold bands replace our original wedding rings. The traditional diamond set lives in my jewelry box. In its place, a beautiful emerald and diamond ring now adorns my left hand. Each time I attend a wedding, I reflect on my personalized symbolism of our vows. An outward expression of mutual fidelity and loyalty, the circular shape represents an eternal love, without beginning or end. As the gold of the ring requires heat and pressure to form the perfect circle, facing adversities of life together bond us as individuals into one. The green of the emerald represents growing love and commitment. Each time I glance at my left hand, I remember our vows.

Decades later, I sat in another church, listened to the preacher, and cherished the memories of my wedding day. My husband and I heard the same sermon. We drove home in relative silence. He retrieved his ring from the bathroom counter that Sunday afternoon and now wears it every day. He no longer says, "It's too big. I'm afraid I'll lose it."

After almost fifty years of marriage, his action assures me of his faithfulness and love. One hot summer afternoon we stood before the minister, our family and friends and recited traditional vows. "With this ring I thee wed, and all my worldly goods I thee endow. In sickness and in health, in poverty or in wealth, till death do us part?"

Neither of us envisioned the challenges we would encounter. When asked the secret for a long and happy marriage, I reply, "Commitment first to God, then to each other and the marriage. Choose to honor the promises and remain faithful regardless of circumstances or emotions."

Pecan Pie Surprise

"This is my invariable advice to people: Learn how to cook- try new recipes, learn from your mistakes, be fearless, and above all have fun!"
Julia Child, My Life in France

"I want to spend Thanksgiving with my family. We see your parents all the time." I fought back the tears as we rehashed the weeklong argument.

"My parents expect us to be with them," Kerry stubbornly held his ground, unmoved by my tears.

Over a few short months, I turned eighteen, graduated from high school, and got married. I knew no one in Dallas except my in-laws. I found myself away from my family for the first time, without friends. When Kerry left for work each morning, I busied myself with making a home of our little apartment. Lonely and bored, I needed something to occupy my time.

To be fair, we treated my homesickness by visiting my family often. A three-hour weekend trip cured my melancholy mood for a while. However, I couldn't imagine not being with my family for the holiday.

"What if we have everyone here? Then we can be with both families." I compromised.

"That could work." Kerry agreed.

We extended the invitation and both our families accepted. Crisis averted.

What possessed me to host Thanksgiving dinner only five months into my marriage?

Confidently, I planned the menu and never questioned my ability to prepare a feast. After all, I excelled in my home economics classes. I attempted all kinds of recipes and rarely failed to turn out an edible, if not scrumptious result. One wedding gift, a Betty Crocker cookbook, provided instructions for the turkey, dressing, and every side dish needed to make a traditional Thanksgiving dinner. No doubt in my mind – I could do this – no problem. I eagerly set out to prove myself and dazzle everyone.

What in the world was I thinking?

I never considered my new mother-in-law's skills in the kitchen. Her cornbread dressing won praise from everyone who tasted it. She excelled at pie baking, especially chocolate and coconut cream pies.

My sister-in-law, Karen Ann, possessed legendary skills in the kitchen. She could've given Paula Dean significant competition. Only her extraordinary sense of humor and comic timing exceeded her culinary proficiency.

I worked all week cleaning, shopping, and baking. As a teenage bride, I needed to impress my parents and my in-laws and demonstrate my responsibility and maturity. I anticipated every detail, wanting the day to be perfect.

Though my younger sisters spent a week with us earlier in the summer, my parents visited our apartment for the first time on Thanksgiving Day. The combined family gathered, twelve of us, packed like sardines into our one bedroom studio apartment.

If I planned the event today, I would ask each person to bring a dish. However, youthful exuberance guided the

1969 Thanksgiving plans. My decision to prepare everything myself set the stage for disaster.

Everyone arrived as scheduled. Lack of space dictated buffet service. The small round table overflowed with every traditional food needed to complete a proper Thanksgiving celebration.

Though we enjoyed a proper Thanksgiving feast, I don't recall the turkey, cornbread dressing, fruit salad, or any of the other dishes from our first Thanksgiving together. I only recall the dessert.

My beautiful pecan pie looked just like the picture in the cookbook, the perfect consistency. Dessert promised to be the crowning achievement of the entire meal. Experience taught me not to attempt piecrust from scratch. Because my previous attempts failed miserably, I purchased a ready-made frozen crust and proceeded to create my masterpiece. The lack of perfection became obvious when I sliced the pecan pie, exposing a culinary failure. A thin film of waxed paper separated the perfect pecan pie filling from the store bought piecrust.

Surprise!

You're Killing Me

"Take it easy driving – the life you save may be mine."
James Dean

In the days of our early marriage, Kerry and I owned a little pale yellow Corvair. The slightly visible, but still recognizable reminder of our wedding day distinguished our Corvair from all others on the road. One of our *brilliant,* (sarcasm intended) friends used purple tempera paint to decorate the car. One-year later close observers still distinguished the words "Just Married" on the hatchback.

Our date nights often consisted of evenings at the drive-in movie theater snuggled in the little yellow car. That is, if Kerry couldn't talk Karen into taking her GTO, which he liked much more than anything he drove during his teenage years. He *seriously* loved Karen's car and bordered on coveting it. Often we double dated with Kerry's sister, Karen, and her husband, Tom. On cold winter nights, Kerry started the car's engine and ran the heater to keep us all warm.

"I smell something funny," Karen commented on more than one occasion.

Kerry retorted, "I don't smell anything, Karen Ann. It's just your imagination."

The constant bickering chatter continued for months during our frequent outings. Karen insisting she smelled something nasty and Kerry equally questioning her sanity.

Buying a new sports car topped Kerry's priority list. My father-in-law advised against the purchase and used his influence to encourage a more practical alternative. However, my 19 year-old husband set aside common sense in favor of the fulfilling the dream of owning a brand new sports car. The first major decision of our young married life ignored caution. He salivated at the sight of the sporty 1969 GTO. Straight off the showroom floor, the sleek Pontiac came fully equipped with everything the factory offered. The color, gold, with a black vinyl top and black interior completed the fantasy. We negotiated the price and arranged financing.

Kerry called his sister and made plans to go to the drive-in. The car evoked the exact response he hoped. He counted on Karen to share his youthful appreciation. She matched his excitement. "Yea! The asphyxiation is over!"

The recall notice arrived one week after we traded our Corvair for the GTO. Chevrolet discovered a carbon monoxide leak from the engine, which happened to be in the rear of the car. Heat for passengers came from air directly passed over the cylinders in the engine. The design flaw contaminated air inside the vehicle when the heater engaged.

As soon as the news story hit the stands, Kerry got a call from his older sister. "I told you I smelled something – I knew you were trying to kill me!"

A Most Nontraditional Holiday

"Love wholeheartedly, be surprised, give thanks and praise... then
you will discover the fullness of your life."
Estonian Proverb

Our family Thanksgiving never resembled the movie portrayal of relatives seated at a perfectly decorated table. More commonly, we set a buffet of our favorite traditional Thanksgiving foods on the kitchen counter. After we loaded holiday paper plates with turkey, cornbread dressing, and all the trimmings, the large family scattered throughout the house and looked for an empty seat to consume our favorite foods. Texas weather typically allowed the children to play outside while the adults visited and watched Dallas Cowboy football.

One year my sisters and I decided to try something different. It worked so well, we continued the tradition for several years. Our families adopted a new tradition. We traveled to various state parks and set up camp for the entire Thanksgiving weekend. With some creative planning, we managed to incorporate all the traditional essentials for a Thanksgiving feast. The extended weekend allowed extra quality time for reconnecting and relaxing around a campfire. These camping excursions allowed bonding of our extended family and created priceless memories.

Our first Thanksgiving in Bluff Dale stands out as particularly memorable. We set up camp on the property that would become our new home. I extended invitations to our extended family including our respective in-laws. On Thanksgiving Day, more than twenty of us gathered in the Mountain Lakes clubhouse. The feast included turkey and dressing with giblet gravy and all the traditional side dishes. Our adult children requested favorite foods, because for one niece Thanksgiving could never be complete without her grandmother's "pink stuff."

Determined to remain true to another long-standing Thanksgiving Day tradition, we brought in a television from the RV. Although no one remembers who won or lost, Dallas Cowboy fans supported their team. A football pot enriched one family member by $10. With full tummies, some dozed off until a cheer from the group disturbed their naps.

"Let's make Christmas ornaments." I directed the children and teens to the table where we spread supplies for angels, Christmas scenes, and other decorations.

The afternoon passed quickly as we worked, talked, laughed, and played together. We looked for every opportunity to document the day in photographs.

Tired from the busy day, some of us headed to our individual campers or tents, while others said good-bye and drove home to their own beds.

How our lives have changed over the years since that gathering!

The family never gathered exactly this way again. Death, illness, and infirmity changed our family. We never anticipated this would be the last holiday we would spend with Kerry's sister, Karen. Before Christmas that year, she died of a heart attack.

Over the decade that followed, Daddy, Mother and Big Daddy joined her in heaven. The extended family no longer resides close enough to carry on the traditional weekend. Distance necessitates new traditions. Still, blessings abound. That special holiday only two children brightened the festivities. Over the next few years, weddings added new in-laws, and the next generation boomed from two to more than twenty and counting.

Shared traditions and memories bond us together. Recall your favorite holidays. Do your recollections focus on the perfectly decorated table or the perfect dinner? Or do your memories, like mine, center on the people you love? Do the quirky stories of your family history make you remember and smile or better yet, laugh aloud?

Holidays stir nostalgic emotions. The smell of the turkey baking in the oven triggers memories of wonderful times. Sweet potatoes topped with marshmallows remind me of my father-in-law. No one makes chocolate pie or cornbread dressing like Maw-Maw. Wistfully reminiscing motivates me to make the best of each family moment we enjoy. This year's holiday soon becomes next year's memory. Our parents passed the torch of tradition and memory making, and soon our generation will pass it on to our children.

I wonder which stories my daughter and her cousins will share about me, their aunts and uncles, and their grandparents. I hope they laugh at the eccentric, bizarre things we did – recall a feeling of warmth and acceptance – recognize my commitment to a strong and abiding faith in

God – and know without a doubt my unconditional love for each of them.

I thank my God every time I remember you. Philippians 1:3

There's Always Room for a Little More

"Insanity: doing the same thing over and over again and expecting different results."
Albert Einstein

On my wedding day, I gained not only a spouse but an extended family as well. I married Kerry only three months after my eighteenth birthday. The eldest of four children, I embraced all the joy, responsibility, and psychosis birth order entails. His parent's only son, Kerry, arrived on the third birthday of his sister, Karen. From the time he was born, she shared everything with him, including her birthday. When I joined the family, she became my older sister. She encouraged me to be less cautious and explore all sorts of mischief.

The two of us discovered a knack for creating situations for ourselves. One of our first adventures as young brides occurred the first summer of our marriage. Along with our husbands, we embarked on a road trip to the border between Texas and Mexico. My father-in-law discouraged the journey. He doubted whether his children possessed the maturity to make the trip. Terrified his children would get into some kind of trouble; he anticipated bailing us out of a Mexican jail and told us so. In hindsight, our youthful exuberance warranted his concern. We disregarded concerns, eagerly planned the trip, and set out to prove to our parents wrong. What could possibly happen?

Both Karen and I lacked a talent for interior design. A tight budget dictated our decorating expenditures. Karen located an outlet, and we planned a shopping excursion to choose furnishings for our respective apartments. We chose an identical Spanish style sofa and matching chair. We both loved the blue and green floral pattern with ornately carved wooden arms. We rationalized, "They'll look totally different in our apartments. We'll add different lamps and tables. Besides, Mom and Dad are the only people who visit both places. It won't make any difference to them. "

We each paid $300 for the set, loaded the monstrosity on a trailer, and transported the purchase to our studio apartment across town. Only one wall in the small apartment accommodated the nine-foot sofa. When Kerry and I stretched out on opposite ends of the sofa, our feet barely touched. The addition of our new purchase accentuated the lack of accessories in our sparsely furnished residence.

Our desire for inexpensive accessories prompted the trip to Laredo, Texas and across the border to Nuevo Laredo, Mexico. Without reservations, we set out Friday afternoon after work. "That looks like a decent place. Let's check it out," we noticed the vacancy sign and decided to stop for the night.

The next morning, we continued to our intended destination. We arrived in Laredo by late afternoon. Karen and I couldn't wait to get across the border, seek out bargains, and add accessories to our 1970s décor. The first afternoon, the four of us explored the border town. None of the group claimed travel experience. "I've never been out of Texas, "I excitedly announced."

Kerry related a story of traveling with his dad to Juarez. "During the summers as a kid, I always played outside and got very dark from being in the sun. Daddy took me on a work trip to Juarez. I begged for a sombrero. He bought a big one that covered my face. When we drove back across the border, the customs officers quizzed me. They asked me my name and my nationality. I was only eight years old, and I didn't understand what they meant. The police officers frightened me. When they continued to question me, Dad forcefully raised his voice. 'Tell them you're an American, Boy!'"

Kerry advised us, "Show your ID. Be polite. We'll be fine."

The next day, we set out with cash in hand to barter and bring home treasures. The guys napped while Karen and I set out on our own. We drove Kerry's pride and joy, the new GTO. While we employed the common sense to park the car on the Texas side and walk across the border, we failed to plan a way to transport our purchases back to the car. Karen purchased an end table and hired a young Mexican boy with "papers" to carry it across the bridge.

We arrived at the car just in time to rescue it from the tow-truck driver. I unknowingly parked the vehicle in a spot reserved for a government official. The police officer allowed us to remove the car without fine. Relieved, I drove back to the hotel. The two of us vowed never to share the near debacle with anyone. I imagined myself waiting for my father-in-law to bail me out of a Mexican jail.

We returned to Nuevo Laredo multiple times over the next few days. Each trip resulted in the deposit of a trunk load of treasures in the motel room. Kerry and I purchased a huge iron chandelier with amber glass globes for our dining room. Karen and Tommy bought tables. We excitedly added miscellaneous treasures until reality sunk in. "How in the world are we going to get this stuff back to Dallas? No way we can fit everything in the trunk of the Pontiac."

Ever practical, Kerry resolved the dilemma, "I saw a U-Haul dealer. We'll rent a trailer to get it all back home."

Karen kept the end table for many years, repainting it a couple of times to match changes in her decor. The chandelier became a part of our dining room in our little studio apartment. When we moved into our first home, it moved with us. When we sold our Oak Cliff cottage, we left the light fixture. After an emotional debate, I agreed to leave behind the vestiges of our early marriage style. "I'll miss this chandelier. It's like a part of the family. I carried it across the border, and it's been with us a really long time."

Decades later, we set out on another shopping adventure. Our Black Friday shopping tradition started one year when we camped at the Mountain Lakes camp ground for Thanksgiving weekend. Karen, along with my sister, Lisa, and my daughter, Ginger, all piled into my car and headed for the mega sales at Wal-Mart. We found amazing bargains and filled four shopping carts with Christmas gifts.

With trepidation, I realized, "No way will all this stuff fit in my Taurus."

We packed in every item possible. I left Lisa and Ginger at Wal-Mart's front door. Karen and I drove back to the R.V Park and unloaded. I returned to Wal-Mart to retrieve a very cold Ginger and Lisa. Wal-Mart declined to allow them back in the store, since they already checked out. I treated them to a well-deserved hot breakfast.

You'd really think after our many misadventures, Karen and I might learn a lesson and consider consequences before we purchased bargains. However, that wasn't the case. Our final shopping trip together turned out to be yet another adventure. Karen phoned me, "Sears has floor jacks on sale for $49. I want to get one for Stephen. Do you think Kerry could use one? It'd make a good Christmas gift."

"Sounds good to me – I'll be over to pick you up in an hour." I excitedly agreed, since I frequently struggled to find a useful gift for my husband.

"This is a great bargain," the sales clerk remarked as he loaded the jacks into my car.

"They're Christmas gifts for my son-in-law and for her husband. Thank you so much for your help," Karen gratefully acknowledged the gentleman.

Proud of our purchases, we returned home. Again, we miscalculated, never considering the weight of our treasures – far too heavy for the two of us to lift from the trunk. Again, we suffered the consequences of our mistake! We paid a neighbor to relocate the jacks into her house. The cost of unloading erased any savings of the bargain purchase.

No matter what kind of fix we found ourselves in, Karen always found a way to make me laugh. We laughed at each other and ourselves. Her infectious laugh diffused serious situations. We created situations and turned them into memories. Those memories comfort me, when I miss my sweet sister.

It's Been a Really Long Time

"Why not seize the pleasure at once, how often is happiness destroyed by preparations, foolish preparations."
Jane Austen

"Okay, girls, let's go. We're due at the Arlington in 20 minutes." I prompted my sister-in-law and daughter.

We traveled to Arkansas for the Fourth of July holiday. While my husband fished with a professional guide, the ladies splurged and scheduled a hot springs bath and massage at the spa. In preparation for the trip, I investigated the history of Hot Springs and the historic hotel.

The Arlington Resort and Spa preserved a colorful history. Since the original opening in 1875, visitors sought the healing waters of Hot Springs. A new, larger facility replaced the original hotel and served guests until it burned in 1923. The current facility opened in 1924 and preserved the history of the original buildings. Throughout its history, the Arlington hosted average, famous, and infamous visitors.

The Arlington's luxurious accommodations and location attracted many famous guests including U.S. presidents Franklin Roosevelt, Harry Truman, George H. W. Bush, and native son, Bill Clinton. Many professional athletes and entertainers relaxed and luxuriated in the thermal baths at the Arlington. The notorious gangster, Al Capone, favored room 442 and reserved the entire fourth floor for his staff and bodyguards.

From the moment we entered the hotel, each detail enhanced our resort experience. The staff directed us to the main elevator, where a uniformed operator greeted us and manually programmed our destination. The elevator, lined with beveled glass and shining brass, heightened our anticipation and promised a lavish encounter.

The door opened and we stepped into a large bathhouse with high ceilings and elongated, opaque windows. The black and white floor tiles and the claw-foot tubs maintained a vintage feel. Our package entitled us to an afternoon of luxurious pampering.

An attendant dressed in a white uniform escorted us to the locker room. We removed our clothing and signaled her when we were ready. She discreetly wrapped us in sheets and accompanied us to the tubs. Water from the natural hot springs filled the bathtubs. Each of us eased into a deep bath of steaming, swirling water. Our aide instructed us to sip a cup of hot water and cover our faces with a warm cloth to enhance the perspiration and remove impurities.

The history of the massive bathhouse intrigued and mesmerized me. I wondered, *Could Eleanor Roosevelt, Barbara Bush, or some celebrated actress have been in this same tub?*

I closed my eyes, detached from the surroundings, and allowed the hot water to wash away the stresses of the past months. When the pre-set timer rang, our personal assistant helped us out of the bath and again wrapped us in a sheet. Warmed, cleansed, and relaxed, we proceeded to the massage room. The massage therapist proficiently performed techniques designed to provide the maximum relaxation and pampering experience.

After the massage, we dressed and returned to the reality of our moderately priced hotel on the lake.

In the privacy of our room, Ginger spoke up, "Was your jet pointed at an odd place?"

"It was really strong. It pushed against my leg at an odd angle. I had a really hard time staying straight in the tub." I responded.

Normally naïve and shy, she uncharacteristically described in detail, though still discreetly, "Mine pointed directly at my private area."

Karen laughed heartily and sighed with deep satisfaction, "Mine, too! OOOOH, YESSS! - It's been a really long time. Where do I sign up again?"

A Pleasant Day in the Garden

God's Garden - Robert Frost
God made a beauteous garden
With lovely flowers strown,
But one straight, narrow pathway
That was not overgrown.
And to this beauteous garden,
He brought mankind to live,
And said, To you, my children,
These lovely flowers I give.
Prune ye my vines and fig trees,
With care my flowers tend,
But keep the pathway open
Your home is at the end.

"We can do this. It'll take planning and finagling, but it's doable," I urged my sisters.

We agreed. Mother needed to get out of the apartment. The conducive, spring temperatures provided a perfect opportunity for an outing in the gardens. "We need to make it happen soon before the summer heat makes being outside unbearable."

We enjoyed spending time together and celebrating Mother's birthday presented us an opportunity. Arranging time in our busy schedules presented a challenge, but we agreed to make it happen. "So we're good for the first Saturday in April? I'll make the arrangements, and we'll talk before then."

The next day I reported to the group, "Okay, we're set. I reserved the golf cart to drive Mom and Kerry through the gardens. They'll get a guided tour. The rest of us can walk. We'll load Mom's wheelchair, so we can push her to the picnic area."

The day arrived. "I hope it doesn't rain – it sure is cloudy and overcast. Did you get a sweater? It could get a little cool." I reminded Mom as I collected her bag.

I mentally reviewed the checklist. Both Kerry and Mom brought jackets. The ice chest in the trunk held a more than adequate picnic lunch. *I think I have everything we could possibly need.*

With considerable effort, we loaded the wheelchair in the trunk and Mother in the front seat of the car. Lisa, Ginger, and Kerry crowded into the back seat of my Taurus. Safely secured, we set out for Clark Gardens in Mineral Wells, Texas.

God, please don't let it rain. We need this day to be perfect. I prayed silently.

The summer and fall of 2007, tested my every reserve. My husband, Kerry, fell from a ladder and sustained a burst fracture of his T-12, L-1. Though he lacked stamina, he miraculously recovered with an ability to walk normally. In the middle of Kerry's recuperation, Daddy died after a three-year battle with lung cancer. Mother and my step-dad, James, deteriorated. Caring for everyone's needs exacted an emotional and physical toll from my sisters and me. Weary, we really needed a day to reconnect and simply enjoy the gardens and each other.

"Where is this place?" Mother asked again.

"We're taking a picnic lunch to Mineral Wells. Patty and Mike are meeting us there. You'll love it, Mom. The flowers are beautiful," I answered patiently.

She couldn't imagine any kind of garden growing in the arid conditions of the West Central Texas community. She rarely ventured out of the house except for physicians visits. Today represented a special treat.

"There's Patty. They beat us here, even though they had further to drive," Mom noted excitedly.

"They're always early. Patty hates to be late," I replied, careful not to contrast my middle sister's prompt nature with Mom's tardy tendencies. *No reason to insert negative sarcasm.*

If James' decision to stay at home disappointed Mother, she never said so. "He hasn't felt well this week. He'd rather stay close to home and watch television," she offered his excuse.

Chemotherapy and radiation robbed my stepfather of his normal energy level. Mom seemed to welcome a break from him and from the apartment. Though we extended the invitation to join us, we gladly accepted his decision to remain at home. Mother's personality brightened out of his presence.

Clark Garden staff welcomed us and helped Mother and Kerry into the golf cart. The speed of the cart thwarted my initial plan to walk beside them and enjoy the tour together. We quickly fell behind and decided to go at our own pace. When the tour completed, we met at the picnic area and spread our feast. *This is worth every minute I spent planning, all the effort, and every penny to see Mom having such a good time.*

"Do we have to go yet? I'd really like to go back and get a closer look at some of the flowers," Mother pleaded.

"Sure. We can take turns pushing the wheelchair," her three daughters agreed.

She seemed more like a little girl, than the elderly woman who occupied the wheelchair. "Granny grew this flower in her yard. I could never get it to grow at my house," she recalled as we stopped at one plant and then another.

What started as a private family garden inspired a botanical oasis. The fifty-acre garden boasted sustainable, low maintenance plants, designed to survive Texas droughts. The wheelchair accessible paths offered flexibility for elderly and disabled individuals to enjoy nature.

Swans and ducks entertained us as we sat beside one of the many water features. The highlight of the afternoon occurred when a beautiful peacock opened his tail feathers and strutted as if to say. "Watch me – Admire me – Am I not the most beautiful creature you've ever seen?"

"It's getting late. We should head home. We need to get home before dark," I reluctantly directed the group to the exit.

Patty guided the wheelchair down the path toward the parking lot. The wheelchair resisted the change in the path's surface. She backed up and sharply punched the wheels over the ridge. The sudden motion catapulted the chair with Mother across the rise in the pavement. Patty jerked the chair back narrowly avoiding a catastrophic collision of our mother with the pavement. Once assured of no damage to Patty, Mother or the wheelchair, we dissolved into fits of laughter.

"That's not the first time you've tried to kill me. Remember the driving lesson?" Mother joked.

Patty and Lisa cackled as they recalled a bloody incident – much funnier in retrospect. "You shouldn't have yelled, *dip*," Patty defended her position.

"I didn't have my license yet, and Mom was teaching me to drive. The three of us were in the front seat of the old Cadillac. Mother sat in the middle. I drove the speed limit, but didn't see the *dip* warning sign. She screamed at the top of her lungs and scared me to death. I hit the brakes and threw her into the mirror."

Mom held pressure on the gash between her eyes. Blood gushed. "Don't look, Lisa!" Patty panicked. "If you pass out, I can't take care of both of you."

Instead of going directly to the emergency room, the trio headed home. Mother removed her blood soaked blouse and discovered a pool of blood in her bra. "I think it's okay," Mom examined her head in the mirror.

As the gaping wound continued to ooze, she reconsidered. "I might need a stitch or two."

"I'll drive you," Patty offered.

"I think it's better if I drive us," Mother collected her purse and keys.

The minor injury healed quickly. Patty eventually learned to drive. All three delighted in retelling the story. Each added her unique perspective to the event, always adding Mother's alternative reason for the accident, "Patty got even with me for grounding her."

"At least this time you don't need stitches," Patty joked as the laughter subsided.

"Wait, we have to get pictures to document our day," all of us talked at once.

"Lean back on your back foot. It makes you look thinner."

"How's that work?"

"That's silly. Who told you that?"

"Whatever – We'll try anything to look skinny."

"We really have to go now if we're going to get home before dark."

Time passed quickly on the drive home as we recalled details and shared our favorite memories of the day. Once back at the apartment, we assisted Mom to her recliner. Clearly exhausted, she closed her eyes and slept before I closed and locked the door.

As my mother aged, every day brought new challenges – dementia, illness, pain. Although some days nothing pleased her, other days she found joy in simplest things. She experienced life with childlike enthusiasm – amazed and amused by everything.

I slept soundly that night, dreaming of a garden. The laughter and love of my family rewarded my endeavor. When I closed my eyes, images flooded my memory. I visualized the beautiful plants and birds of the garden and recalled the sweet aroma of the flowers. Raucous laughter of my mother and sisters rang in my ears. We enjoyed a pleasant day in the garden – indeed – a very pleasant day.

Reflections on life lessons

"Forget what hurt you in the past, but never forget what it taught you. However, if it taught you to hold onto grudges, seek revenge, not forgive or show compassion, to categorize people as good or bad, to distrust and be guarded with your feelings then you didn't learn a thing. God doesn't bring you lessons to close your heart. He brings you lessons to open it, by developing compassion, learning to listen, seeking to understand instead of speculating, practicing empathy and developing conflict resolution through communication. If he brought you perfect people, how would you ever learn to spiritually evolve?"
Shannon L. Alder

The Reality of a Delusional World

"My favorite vacation spot now, is the place in my mind where my best memories of you are kept."
Marie Botonis *When Caring Takes Courage*

"Do what you need to do to protect yourself and your staff. Use your best judgement. Call the police if you feel it's necessary," Lisa advised the nursing home administrator.

The deterioration of Mother and James' physical and mental health necessitated a move to a facility capable of providing medical care. We all understood the difficult adjustment facing our family. However, nothing in our life experience prepared us for the ugly side of dementia.

"I need help to care for your mother. I am getting weaker and can't take care of her by myself. My cancer is getting worse, and I want her to be settled before something happens to me. Will you girls promise me you'll take care of your mother? Can you help me find a place for us?" James determined to arrange for Mother's care.

We checked out the local facilities and took James to visit. He discussed the options with Mother and made the final decision. "We're ready to make the move," they assured us.

We packed, vacated their apartment, and relocated them to the nursing home. We expected a difficult transition, but none of us truly understood the complex issues.

Though we'd seen signs of instability, neither my sisters nor I anticipated the coming storm. We listened to vague complaints about the food and confinement. We watched as signs of unrest exacerbated to a destructive toronado.

James controlled the couple's finances, and money represented security and independence to him. The complicated Medicare/Medicaid regulations confused him. In his mind, the nursing home robbed him and kept him hostage. He held the administrator responsible.

One particularly difficult morning, he marched into the business office and demanded his money. Attempts to reason with the irrational patient failed. The more they talked, the more agitated the resident became. He stormed out of the office and out the back door. He retrieved a chain from his truck, returned to the lobby, and threatened the staff.

While the social worker tried to diffuse the situation, the manager phoned Lisa. Recent verbal confrontations confirmed the family's inability to control our step-father's behavior. Though he and Mother agreed on the move, they often blamed Lisa and me for their circumstances.

The family discussed the situation and determined to allow the professionals to make necessary medical decisions. "What's it going to take? Perhaps the medical staff will evaluate and provide medications to help."

The police arrived and restored sanity to a chaotic scene. The threat of jail shocked the hotheaded elderly man back to reality.

Over the next few days, a psychiatrist visited and prescribed medication. We never discussed the incident. We acted as if we knew nothing of the episode.

Though they frequently complained, life settled into an easy rhythm. They connected with favorite staff members. James became known as a jokster and teased with caregivers.

The couple cared for each other. She made sure he got his favorite foods. He made sure the nurses attended to Mom's needs.

When I visited one afternoon, Mother showed me her freshly painted nails. "Look, they got polish on my cuticles. I could do a better job," she declared.

"I'm sure you could, Mom. I bet you still know how to give the best manicure. You always did a great job." I praised her.

"They asked me if I'd like to paint the ladies' nails next week," she added.

"You should, Mom. It'll be fun. You'll make their hands look pretty," I encouraged.

The next week I found Mother and James in their room preparing for dinner. They excitedly announced. "We are so lucky – We get to live where we work."

Huh? Confused, I wondered as she continued.

Mother spent the afternoon manicuring the resident's nails. I'm not sure what job James imagined.

However, they both excitedly discussed how fortunate they felt to have such wonderful jobs. With the best bonus of all – A nice place to live.

The fantasy only lasted a few days. For a short while, the interlude broke the monotony and made them incredibly happy. I marveled at their ability to immerse themselves in the same delusion. Everyone around them happily played along. Much better to have a happy employee than a potential criminal with a chain.

Lost and Found
The Mystery of the Missing Keys

"I wish I could lose weight as easy as I lose my keys, pen, cell phone, my temper, and even my mind."
Unknown

"I found someone who wants to buy James' truck. Her mother is Mom's nurse," Lisa told me.

"Did you find the keys?" I asked.

"Not yet. I don't know where else to look. We've turned the room upside down, looked in every pocket, every drawer, everywhere I can imagine. If they don't turn up by Monday, I'm calling a locksmith," she replied.

"It'll be worth it. I know it is bothering Mom. Every time she looks out the window, it's a reminder. James is gone," I agreed.

James loved his Ford pick-up. He bought his pride and joy fresh off the showroom floor. He cared for it more lovingly than any other possession – perhaps even more lovingly than friends and family. He kept the keys in his pocket all the time. Though he hadn't driven the truck for more than a year, the keys represented the last vestiges of his independence.

He stubbornly refused to relinquish the keys to the staff or to any family member. We worried he might try to escape with Mother, drive away and not be able to find his way home. Eventually, he no longer spoke of running away. Yet, he still diligently guarded the truck keys.

After the memorial service, we cleared everything from the room. Mother kept a few personal items and dispersed the rest of her husband's belongings to friends and family members. She chose special items to give to caregivers who had been especially kind to them.

No matter how thoroughly we searched, the illusive keys remained missing. *Where did he hide them? Could we have possibly missed them when we packed up the clothes?*

"We've prayed for God to send a buyer for the truck. God knows where those keys are. Let's ask Him to help us find them," my sister and I agreed.

Mother's mail arrived on Monday morning. She opened a package from Brookshire's Grocery and to her amazement found a set of Ford truck keys.

How the keys found their way to Brookshire's home office remains a mystery. Inquiring minds couldn't let it go without a reasonable explanation.

During the last months of his life, James became increasingly confused. The oncologist suggested an MRI to determine whether the colon cancer invaded his brain. Lisa drove him to the imaging center.

"He must have left the keys at the imaging center. The technicians required him to remove all metal objects during testing. I bet he left the keys in the locker," we reasoned.

We imagined the clinic staff discussions. The keys offered no clues to the identity of the owner. Only a single Brookshire's reward card accompanied the solitary Ford key. A staff member proposed, "What if we send the keys to

Brookshire's? They can scan it and find an address for the owner."

Brookshire's mailed the key ring to the address on file, the couple's old apartment address. Forwarded mail containing the keys reached Mother at the nursing home hours before Lisa called the locksmith.

The months following James' death proved challenging for Mother. The smallest details distressed her. The lost keys and the sale of the truck represented the last unresolved business. The small package arrived at exactly the right time. Some people might consider the event a coincidence. I choose to accept it as an example of how God cares for the things that concern us – even an unidentified set of Ford truck keys.

Models of Courage
Lessons from Women of Character

"Godly character is not defined in the good times but the tough times. Our responses reflect our character.
If all could just see Jesus in us."
Josh McDowell

I learned survival skills from some amazingly strong women. Each one played a vital role in my development. I honor each as an example of what it means to be a Godly woman.

My mother modeled the value of hard work. She operated a beauty salon. She placed value on her ability to convey importance to each patron. I spent long hours at the salon watching Mom meet the individual needs of each lady. She taught me to respect myself and value others.

Granny Carr, my maternal grandmother, introduced me to the joys of living in the country. I spent many summers following her as she went about her daily chores. I learned about vegetable and flower gardening, preserving produce, cooking, and gathering eggs, just to name a few of many practical lessons. Terrified, I watched as she wrung the neck of a chicken. As a young widowed mother, she learned to be self-sufficient. When she met and married my grandfather, they modeled a committed marriage. Together they built a life as a blended family, loving and appreciating each other and their family.

When Popo Dooly died, my paternal grandmother, Momo, left the farm where they worked together as sharecroppers. She lovingly provided a home and cared for her mother until her death at age 96. She then became the caregiver for my younger siblings and me. She exhibited a spirit of selflessness, which I learned to appreciate as an adult. I often failed to show her the respect she deserved. She placed little value on material wealth and taught me the value of being content in all circumstances.

I owe an eternal debt of gratitude to Mama Linda, my stepmother, for bringing about reconciliation between my father and his children. From the moment she met my father, Linda made sure Daddy attended every important event in our lives. She and my dad loved each other very much. His happiness remained her greatest priority. She dedicated herself to making his last years happy ones. From them I learned to value every day, living life to the fullest.

I wonder what Melba Strange thought when her nineteen-year-old son announced he was going to marry me. I was barely eighteen when Melba became my mother-in-law. As a young bride, I behaved immaturely and sometimes irrationally. However, never once, did she criticize me or point out my inadequacies. I loved being around her. Her infectious laugh encouraged everyone to join her. Over the years, she showed me unconditional love and acceptance. She encouraged me to be all God created me to be. I miss her every day.

The day after our wedding Kerry took me to meet his maternal grandmother, Grandmommy Cargile. When her husband died in an accident, a young, pregnant widow moved to Commerce, Texas, and opened a boarding house for students and teachers at East Texas State. She defined the role of single mother, raising seven children. From the nursing home, she continued to serve as the beloved matriarch of a large extended family. I once heard my mother-in-law remark that she never heard her mother say a negative word about anyone. What an amazing compliment! She used her gifts of encouragement and writing to minister to family and friends throughout her life. As I discovered letters and cards she wrote during that time, her words continue to minister to me.

None of these women ever sought the spotlight. They quietly lived lives of integrity. As a tribute, I seek to follow their example and pass on their legacy.

Who can find a virtuous woman?
For her price is far above rubies.
Proverbs 31:10 (KJV)

Remember Who You Are

Lessons from Mother

"Believe in yourself! Have faith in your abilities! Without a humble but reasonable confidence in your own powers, you cannot be successful or happy. "
Norman Vincent Peale

Who is that woman looking back at me from the mirror? The reflection resembles my mother more and more as I age. I hear her words involuntarily escaping my lips – some words of wisdom – others caustic comments of a critical spirit. I choose to emulate her generosity, her passion for helping others, and her love of music.

Over the years, I observed destructive behaviors. Actions and attitudes exacted a toll on her emotional and physical health. I strive to break the cycle of negative health habits, fault finding, critical spirit, and deep seeded bitterness.

My mother dropped out of high school, married my father, and before her eighteenth birthday delivered her first child. Over the next decade, she gave birth to two more daughters and one son.

Though she struggled with the academic skills of reading, writing, and spelling, she found her niche as a cosmetologist. She passionately pursued her career. She demonstrated extraordinary skills. She enjoyed mentoring young beauticians and helping them develop their talents. Typical of mid-century beauty shops, Wanda's Salon of

Beauty welcomed customers for unhurried hours of pampering. She delighted in making her patrons look beautiful. She found ways to highlight the inner beauty in each person who sat in her chair. She spoiled them, making each person feel special.

She championed the underdog. Young single mothers with small children often found their way to her door. She offered employment and a hand-up. If the young family needed a place to stay, she opened our home until the woman got back on her feet. Even though we didn't have a lot, she readily shared. Growing up during the depression taught her how to stretch food – enough to feed a crowd. As miraculously as Christ feeding the five-thousand, Mother and Daddy prepared and served available food. Though they struggled to provide necessities, no one ever left the table hungry.

As much sympathy as she extended to the down and out, Mom expressed little tolerance for people she described as uppity. She showed disdain for the snobbish elite of the community. Her caustic, critical tirades clearly communicated her opinions of injustices she witnessed. She often judged a situation without knowing the whole story. I frequently heard her quote a cliché comment, "I wish I could buy her for what she's worth and sell her for what she thinks she's worth."

Mom showed little patience for my introverted nature, which exaggerated normal teenage insecurities. Though I worked hard and excelled academically, I spent most of my teen years feeling inferior and excluded. In reality, I isolated and excluded myself until I learned to reach beyond my comfort zone, discover my passion, and find my own voice.

In her unique way, Mother encouraged me. She proudly acknowledged her talents and encouraged her children to explore our passions. When I tearfully recounted my adolescent stories of feeling out of place, she would say, "Always remember, everyone is important. They put their pants on the same way you do – one leg at a time. You are just as good as everyone else. By the same standard, you are no better than anyone else. Treat everyone with the respect they deserve."

Mother taught me well. I learned from her example how to serve others. I learned to be comfortable in my own skin. I discovered an ability to thrive in all kinds of professional and social situations.

I am definitely my mother's daughter. I bristle at injustice and stand up for the disenfranchised. Helping others provides my greatest satisfaction. Being confident in my own abilities allows me to appreciate the abilities of others. Respect for individuals and celebration of their unique gifts creates the atmosphere of acceptance. Every person I encounter offers something of value and adds an interesting dimension to my life.

Mother embraced a simple philosophy of life and encouraged her children to follow her example. *Love your neighbor as you love yourself.* The hidden message in this belief – in order to love your neighbor as yourself, you must first learn to love yourself – an essential lesson I wish I'd learned much sooner.

Saving the Best for Last
Lessons from Daddy

"While women weep, as they do now – I'll fight. While little children go hungry – I'll fight. While men go to prison, in and out, in and out, as they do now -- I'll fight. While there is a drunkard left, while there is a poor lost girl upon the streets, where there remains one dark soul without the light of God—I'll fight! I'll fight to the very end!"
William Booth, founder of the Salvation Army

"Leaving so soon?" I asked as Daddy and Linda collected their coats and said their goodbyes to the family.

"It's getting late and we need to be home before dark."

"You're welcome to spend the night. We have an extra bed."

"The Red Kettle drive starts tomorrow. I have to be there early to collect donations," Dad stated as if he spoke of any other routine task.

"How did you get involved with the Salvation Army?" I inquired.

He talked easily about the area ministerial alliance connecting him to a number of volunteer activities. While he performed a number of duties as the co-pastor of a small community church, the mission of Salvation Army Bell Ringers provided the greatest personal satisfaction. He shared personal stories of assisting families through the local chapter. The practice of raising money and providing Christmas for needy families clearly provided meaning to his holiday experience.

More than a century earlier, before volunteers rang bells at the doors of retail establishments, the Salvation Army reached out to the poor and disenfranchised. William Booth and his wife, Catherine, walked the streets of London and preached to the poor, homeless, hungry, and destitute. Following its inception in 1852, the ministry grew and expanded to other countries including the United States.

The needs of the poverty-stricken in San Francisco distressed Salvation Army Captain Joseph McFee. Without regard to funding the project, he committed to provide a free

> **Salvation Army's mission statement:**
>
> The Salvation Army, an international movement, is an evangelical part of the universal Christian Church. Its message is based on the Bible. Its ministry is motivated by the love of God. Its mission is to preach the gospel of Jesus Christ and to meet human needs in His name without discrimination.

Christmas dinner for one thousand destitute individuals. As he prayed for a solution to the overwhelming task, he remembered his sailor days in Liverpool, England. Sailors arriving at Stage Landing tossed a coin or two into Simpson's pot, a large iron kettle, to help the poor. Inspired by the recollection, Captain McFee placed a similar pot on Market Street. Beside the iron kettle, a sign read, "Keep the Pot Boiling." The money tossed into the kettle provided a proper Christmas meal. As promised, volunteers fed the hungry on Christmas Day 1891.

Captain McFee's idea launched The Red Kettle tradition that spread not nationwide but all across the world. Modern Salvation Army Red Kettle donations provide Thanksgiving and Christmas for more than four million otherwise forgotten people.

As a young man, my dad felt God leading him to ministry. Amity Baptist Church ordained and licensed him. He enrolled in classes at Hardin Simmons University in Abilene, Texas. When the demands of providing for a wife and children took priority, he dropped out of school. The goal of serving as a pastor seemed unattainable. Perhaps he questioned his call. Satan used circumstances to discourage and discredit him. When his marriage failed, he assumed he couldn't serve as pastor. He abandoned any ministerial plans.

A plumbing company offered him a position as a plumber's helper. He showed an aptitude for the trade, obtained his license, and worked the majority of his life in the plumbing trade. Perhaps he could serve God by living his values in the secular work place.

A major change occurred when he and his second wife, Helen, decided to attend the small community church near their lake home. His recent retirement from a Dallas plumbing company left him searching for purpose in the next phase of his life. When the minister of the church resigned, the congregation approached Daddy. Slowly, confidence and compassion replaced insecurities and self-doubt. He built a network of colleagues who recognized and nurtured his unique gifts.

George and granddaughters:
Ginger, Kristen, Diane, Angela, Jenni, Elizabeth, Amber

I observed at a distance as he involved himself in church and community service. The Red Kettle ministry and his local church provided him with opportunities to share God's love.

My father taught me by example the value of serving others. When many of his peers retired to lives of self-indulgence, he chose to spend his final years caring for the physical and spiritual needs of his community. When Daddy renewed his commitment to follow God's purpose, he gained renewed passion. The joy of life returned. He embraced his purpose, and his winter years proved the happiest, most productive season of my father's life.

Salvation Army Red Kettle volunteers remind me of my Daddy's commitment. I recall the enthusiasm in Daddy's voice as he described his role. He beamed as he shared stories of changed lives and children's dreams fulfilled.

Each time I drop a donation into one of the red kettles, I silently honor my dad. *This one's for you, Daddy.*

"You'll likely not go wrong here if you keep remembering that our Master said, you're far happier giving than getting."
Acts 20:35, The Message

A Memorable Mother's Day Tea

"A mother is not a person to lean on,
but a person to making leaning unnecessary."
Dorothy Fisher

"I asked if I could have more than one guest for the Mother's Day Tea," Mother proudly announced.

Two of her three daughters lived close enough to attend the special event hosted by the nursing home staff. She anxiously anticipated the special event and proudly announced to all of her friends "My girls will be here for tea."

Mother chose her favorite outfit, a bright pink blouse with matching slacks. With the help of the nursing assistants, she carefully styled her hair and applied her make-up. She waited eagerly for my sister and me to arrive.

The staff transformed the usual dining room to a festive tearoom atmosphere. Fine china and a beautiful centerpiece decorated each table. Smiling attendants escorted us to our tables and served a special menu of finger sandwiches and teacakes. A pianist played the residents' favorite tunes and provided additional ambiance.

Mom relished the new experience. She loved her southern style iced tea but never tasted hot tea or traditional teatime treats. She absorbed every detail.

The challenges of the past year faded as we shared a sweet experience.

While her husband lived, the two of them remained isolated in their room and rarely participated in social activities. In the months since his death, Mother engaged fully in the activities, even manicuring the fingernails of some of the residents. She enjoyed musical entertainment of the visiting ensembles and choirs. She joined friends at their assigned dinner table each night. Her personality blossomed, and her social circle enlarged. She particularly enjoyed introducing her children and grandchildren to her new friends.

Several months earlier, a group of friends and I sang at Harbor Lakes. While I sang gospel standards, many of the residents including my mother sang along. Later my friend shared, "Wanda, I wish you could have seen your mother's face. She beamed. She was so proud of you."

The encouraging words of my friend touched me and started a healing process. Over the years, I sought to win my mother's approval but never felt assured of her unconditional love.

A shared experience of a simple tea party provided an affirmation of her love and pride. She spoke of each of her children in loving terms and beamed with pride as she boasted of our accomplishments to her friends and to the staff.

The afternoon passed quickly with pleasant conversation and ended much sooner than Mother wanted. The priceless memory of a 2011 Mother's Day tea brings a sweet smile to my face. I visualize Mother, excitedly experiencing the tea party and enjoying the company of her girls. She introduced us to everyone who stopped to listen as she spoke of all her children and grandchildren.

Five months later, Mother slipped from this world and took her flight to Heaven. Memories of happy times we shared comfort my heart. I look forward to the day we celebrate Mother's Day in Heaven.

Honoring parents involves much more than obedience and caring for them. By becoming a person of character – the daughter or son a parent celebrates and speaks of with pride – we bring honor to the parents who raised us.

A mother's daughters (and sons and grandchildren)
are her treasures.
Author Unknown

The Mansion's Not Ready Yet

"Let not your heart be troubled: ye believe in God, believe also in me. In my Father's house are many mansions: if it were not so, I would have told you. I go to prepare a place for you. And if I go and prepare a place for you, I will come again, and receive you unto myself; that where I am, there ye may be also."
Jesus Christ – John 14: 1-3 KJV

Preoccupied with family demands as I drove to work in September 2007, I searched the sky for inspiration and comfort from God. My father's struggle with cancer consumed my thoughts. Diagnosed with stage IV lung cancer, Daddy fought valiantly and amazed even his oncologist.

He shared his faith with the physician and the oncology staff, "I don't think my doctor understands me," Daddy told me. "I told him – I'll take your medicine, but God's in control. I'll live until God's ready for me to die."

He repeatedly assured his family and friends, "When God is ready for me to go, I'll go. I am ready when He is ready for me. Not until."

For three years, he received multiple chemotherapy regimens and responded positively to each treatment. He continued to live every day fully. When the last drug failed to arrest the growth, the doctor offered no other options and recommended hospice care. Over a matter of a few weeks, Dad's health deteriorated rapidly.

As I drove that September morning, I begged God. I earnestly sought God's ultimate healing and the relief of Daddy's pain and prolonged suffering, "Father God, be merciful. Please don't let Daddy linger."

Bright white clouds divided the vivid blue sky. They formed one single line reaching across the sky moving steadily upward. I imagined the line of clouds as a road connecting the earth to heaven. I thought about the journey. One step at a time, continuing upward until the gates of heaven open, and Christ welcomes his followers inside.

I often prayed during the last days of my father's illness, "God, I know Daddy's ready. Why is this suffering prolonged? What is he waiting for? Please, welcome him home to heaven."

God's promise to prepare a place for believers comforted my heart. I read John 14 regularly. As I meditated on Jesus' words, I chuckled to myself. *The interior decorators must be very busy. They're putting the finishing touches on the mansion. Things have to be perfect for the move in date.*

By the end of September 2007, Daddy inherited his mansion. In the decade following that autumn morning, I walked through the dying process with so many precious souls – my stepfather, my mother, friends, family, and patients. Jesus promised to prepare the mansion. I claimed the sweet assurance of a perfectly prepared mansion for each of them. I imagined no better interior decorator.

The longer I live, and the more losses I experience, the more precious the promise of heaven becomes. Scripture promises something far better than a mansion. "He will wipe every tear from their eyes. There will be no more death, or mourning or crying or pain, for the old order of things has passed away." Revelation 21:4 KJV

Throughout history, ancient societies emphasized the importance of heirs. For the Jews, the birthright of the eldest son entitled him to a double portion of the parental inheritance. While this position afforded special privileges, it required him to fulfill certain responsibilities. This concept continued throughout history. Parents bequeathed property and possessions to their children.

Some families continued to bestow monetary blessings to their heirs. Others, like my extended family, received an entirely different kind of birthright. No individual achieved material wealth. Instead, our ancestors struggled to provide necessities of life. They lived and worked in an agricultural society to supply food and shelter for the family. Their children pursued other career paths and raised their own families.

Our ancestors exhibited hard work and solid character. Their service in the Revolutionary War, Civil War, and World War II displayed patriotism. They provided examples of facing adversity with grace and courage. Imperfect people, they made mistakes – lots of them. However, they lived life – sometimes with great difficulty. They simply lived daily and did the best they could.

Family shapes us into the people we become. We inherit much from our ancestors. Examinations of old photos reveal physical similarities – like hair and eye color or perhaps stature. Genetics predispose us to familial diseases. We mimic habits, sometimes to our consternation.

A wise heir incorporates the strengths of family members and benefits from the mistakes of the past. Author Wynne McLaughlin wrote, "Maybe history wouldn't have to repeat itself if we listened once in awhile."

Faith in God guided the lives of our parents and grandparents. Likely, none of them contemplated their legacy. Yet the values they modeled influenced generations.

They unintentionally bequeathed a priceless legacy – a legacy of love, tenacity, and faith.

The boundary lines have fallen for me in pleasant places; surely, I have a delightful inheritance.

Psalm 16:6 NIV

References

I spent multiple hours examining books, historical and land records.
The staff at the museums, libraries, and government buildings proved invaluable.
Abilene Public Library – Genealogy Section
Anson Public Library
Anson County Court House
Bosque County Archives and Museum
Merkel Area Museum
Merkel Area History – edited by Pat and Larry Gill

Internet resources provided historical supportive data
Abilene Businesses That Are Gone But Not Forgotten |
A Centennial History of Texas Baptists, Broadman Press, 1936)
www.bigcountrycamp.com/about/ourhistory
blogs.ancestry.com/ancestry/2014/10/13/migration-to-america-in-the-1700s/
cinematreasures.org/theaters/16328
facebook group – Remember Abilene When
garisonfitch.com/
germany.travel/en/ms/german-originality/heritage/timeline/timeline.html
historyplace.com/worldhistory/famine/america.htm
Highlights in the History of the Army Nurse Corps Edited by Carolyn M. Feller Lieutenant Colonel, ANC, USAR and Constance Moore Major, ANC U.S Army Center of Military History Washington, D.C., 1995)
homepages.rootsweb.ancestry.com/%7Ebrobst/chronicles/chap2.htm
hornedlizards.org)
ic.galegroup.com/ic/uhic/ReferenceDetailsPage/ReferenceDetailsWindow?zid=a1bdd01f59dacbddab4e6bea68b2a54e&action=2&documentId=GALE%7CCX3436800018&userGroupName=gray02935&jsid=f6ef0c62ec142c368bfc2a12c90b49ea
ilw.com/articles/2001,0817-AILF.shtm

library.uta.edu/digitalgallery/items/browse?page=92&sort_field=Dublin+Core%2CTitle&sort_dir=a

loc.gov/rr/european/imde/germchro.html

.lynnheidelberg.org/beginnewlife.html

.northcarolinaghosts.com/mountains/legend-tom-dooley-scary-truth.php

norway.org/News_and_events/Embassy/Norwegian-American-Organizations/Norwegian_Americans/#.V6PCoqI2fbg

prezi.com/aype3ls1ri44/irish-immigration-to-the-us-in-the-late-1800s/

www.reporternews.com/lifestyle/faith-and-values/methodists-feeding-hungry-needy-at-former-local-restaurant-ep-1182012763-348157851.html

swissinfo.ch/eng/when-the-swiss-made-america/6784658

tpwd.texas.gov)

tshaonline.org)

ushistory.org/us/25f.asp

vintagekidstuff.com/GAUX/gaux.html

wikipedia.org/wiki/Tom_Dula